T0368499

CANCER:
Our Journey

Love, Grief, and Healing in Lockdown

DIANE HUGHES

AuthorHouse™ UK
1663 Liberty Drive
Bloomington, IN 47403 USA
www.authorhouse.co.uk
UK TFN: 0800 0148641 (Toll Free inside the UK)
UK Local: 02036 956322 (+44 20 3695 6322 from outside the UK)

Because of the dynamic nature of the Internet, any web addresses or links contained in this book may have changed since publication and may no longer be valid. The views expressed in this work are solely those of the author and do not necessarily reflect the views of the publisher, and the publisher hereby disclaims any responsibility for them.

This book is printed on acid-free paper.

ISBN: 978-1-6655-9498-1 (sc)
ISBN: 978-1-6655-9499-8 (e)

Print information available on the last page.

Published by AuthorHouse 12/13/2021

authorHOUSE®

Contents

Introduction: My Lovely, Funny, Brave Kevin

'Life is difficult. Is that the word for what I'm feeling - difficult? I'm putting on my PJs and start to feel sad. I want to start crying but can't as Kevin is in the next room, in his office. So I don't cry; I crease my face into a smile and shout, 'What are we going to watch on TV tonight?' (April 2018)

My husband, my best friend, my everything — we are complete together.

I wrote this book because I wanted to share my thoughts and feelings about our journey with cancer. Share the struggles and challenges. During the diary, I write as if I am sometimes talking to Kevin, and other times talking to myself about him. If this is your journey, too, you are not alone. You may relate to this book or you may not. Or it may give you a glimpse of what may be ahead, or not. It is about trying to be positive, stoic, and resilient, or not. During this time, the country went into pandemic lockdown, so two or three weeks after Kevin's funeral, not only was I grieving, I was grieving in lockdown. I was really, really on my own. Perhaps readers can identify with some or all of this—losing someone through cancer, grief in lockdown, or being alone in lockdown.

I almost gave up on publishing my 'diary' because during the move to Formby, while unplugging the desktop, and then setting up again, three months of writing had disappeared. I was upset because I knew I could not remember what I had written in that time, and felt it was not to be. I did pass the hard drive to a techy professional to see if it could be found. I remember driving to work talking to Kevin saying that if it is not found then that is a sign I should not publish it. Those lost three months of writing were found.

Thank you to family and friends who have kindly read this in advance of publication. Following are some of their reactions:

'Real-life reference for anyone in a similar position.'

'What an emotional powerful read—raw, emotional roller coaster that awful numbing pain you describe after Kevin died, the fear and sadness leading up to his death, the almost disbelief and denial that he was dying. The sense of feeling unable to get things done or ease his pain and fear, fighting red tape–type issues is palpable. And the uplifting moments, the memories of love, the beloved dogs, and family, and the support from friends, it all adds up to a very gripping and moving account of your journey with cancer.'

'I wasn't able to put it down for three and a half hours; and yes, a few tears later I had read it all.'

'It really is a beautiful piece of writing and very honest, sincere, moving, funny, and ultimately a testament to enduring love, not just the love you have for Kevin, but also family and your girls.'

'It's written in such a lovely way, and I'm sure it will be a great help to many people. It's a great read and many great memories. I just find it hard because it's so close to my heart. You and Kevin are a huge part of my life.'

1

Our Life Together

When and How We Met

It was November 1991, and we were both at a mutual friend's wedding at Staines Rugby Club. I was there with a boyfriend who disappeared off for ages, talking to other friends. I didn't really know other people there, so I was just standing around. Kevin was there with his sister, Elaine, who went off to talk to friends. So we were both alone, and our eyes met across a crowded room. I went over to Kevin and said, 'Hiya' (Scouse for hello). We lost track of time and seemed to talk for most of that evening. Kevin gave me his work business card as he left, which had his contact telephone number on it. It was only when I finished with 'the boyfriend' in March 1992 that I phoned the number on the card. The operator told me Kevin no longer worked there, but she knew him and would contact him to give him my details. How lucky was that – fate. And the rest is history.

When I met Kevin, he was a T4 paraplegic confined to a wheelchair after a motorbike accident in 1985, he was twenty-three when he had the accident.

Making a Home in Ottershaw

We moved into Ottershaw, Surrey, in March 1993 and made a life. (We had never heard of Ottershaw, which during our time there, we found that not many people had. It's a little village in Surrey, outside the M25, in a countryside setting). We loved going to the local social club, where we met many special friends over the years. We enjoyed fun times with Margaret and Colin (Kevin's mum and dad), playing cards and having laughs. My dad, Tom, came twice a year for two weeks each time, again magical times. All the family from Liverpool and Leeds visited, creating many, many memories. The Haven, the name of our home in Ottershaw for twenty eight years, was always open for a party, poker, drinks, food, and many laughs.

But with a lot of family up north, we decided in 2015, before we got too old to start a new life, to move to the north-west coastal area. We both wanted to live by the beach, near the sea. In Ottershaw, we got down to Brighton as often as we could because we loved the coast. We relocated up north in June 2017, making a sad farewell to a whole life but looking forward to an exciting new start. We did not know then what was about to hit us.

From Engagement to Honeymoon

Kevin proposed to me on Christmas Eve 1993. It was the first Christmas in our new home and the start of our Christmas Eve tradition—roaring fire, salmon butty (Scouse for sandwich), and a glass of sherry as Christmas Eve became Christmas Day.

We enjoyed life. We married on 4 August 2002. It was raining, but it was a beautiful, happy day. I mention the rain because it rained the day I said farewell to Kevin, and to me, those are the opening and closing chapters of our life together. The rain did not dampen our beautiful, happy wedding day, and it made me smile for a moment at Kevin's farewell.

We toured the south-west, Devon and Cornwall, for our honeymoon. We visited the Eden Project, enjoying Cornish pasties and pints and cream teas (the latter a particular love of Kevin's), and drinking champagne as the sun set over Fistral Beach.

How We Spent Holidays

We had many lovely holidays together in Florida, Canada, Las Vegas, New York, and other locations.

Our first holiday together was to Tenerife in September 1992. It will always be a special place with special memories for us—for me now. We swam in the hotel pool late one night (when it was closed) and got told off by security! It was no mean feat because Kevin had to transfer onto the pool hoist, and I had to lower him into the water. Security was thankfully slow.

We had our first cruise in January 1998, to the Caribbean, and we were smitten with cruising. Then Casablanca, Madeira, the Canaries, the Panama Canal, Amsterdam and Guernsey, the Mediterranean, Renaissance and the Rivieras, Rotterdam, Le Havre and Bruges, Belgium. Our final cruise was the fjords in August 2013.

Between cruising and flying abroad, we enjoyed holidays in the United Kingdom. In the Lake District—a beautiful area—we stayed at the Beatrix Potter Hotel. We ate ice cream overlooking Lake Coniston and took a boat trip on Windermere. We visited Norfolk and went to the Sandringham Chapel. But it was not wheelchair accessible at the time, so Kevin waited outside for me. When I returned, there was a woman in a wheelchair right next to him. Kevin said her husband thought it was a parking lot for wheelchairs and had left her next to him while he went into the chapel alone. The look on Kevin's face was to be seen! We both laughed after we had moved away from her.

We went to South Wales, across the Severn Bridge. At that time you had to pay to get into Wales, but it was free to get out. We managed to see most of it during our touring holiday, so we didn't need to go back☺.

Kevin had overcome challenges that arose from his paraplegia before we met, and then we overcame challenges together. We lived life to the full. We enjoyed being with family and friends. But most of all, we enjoyed being with each other and with our dogs, Skip, Sky, Layla, and Bess.

Cancer: Diary Log, 30 March 2018–8 February 2020

Good Friday, 30 March 2018

Kevin was unwell with diarrhoea and sickness towards the end of March. We left it for a few weeks, Kevin kept thinking he would be ok, but on the thirtieth, we went to A&E at Whiston Hospital. We saw the doctor, and Kevin was admitted. Kevin had a scan on Saturday, the thirty-first, which showed an appendix problem. Kevin had keyhole surgery to remove his appendix on Easter Sunday and was discharged on Easter Monday, 2 April. We felt everything was OK now.

Wednesday, 11 April

Ten to eleven days later, Kevin was still not well. We went back to Whiston A&E and another nine-hour wait!, was seen and had tests. Kevin was then moved to a ward for more tests over next few days.

Friday, 13 April

We were given the devastating news that Kevin had bowel cancer.

I was going to the hospital at lunchtime that day and then on to work for an afternoon shift as we thought it was something related to the appendix and would be sorted, so there would be no need for me not to go to work. We were *not* expecting this news.

The doctor had already told Kevin the news about two minutes before I arrived, and he was crying when I entered his room. They said there was a letter in the post (it must have crossed over as we came back to A&E on the eleventh) to say they found cancer cells in his appendix, so they were calling him back in.

How a 'normal' day can turn into a nightmare. Sitting there crying with Kevin, not knowing what to do, not believing this is happening - *It can't be.*

Sunday, 15 April

Kevin has a major bowel operation to remove the tumour and the right part of his bowel. The surgeon told us that if the tumour had got any bigger, it would have attached itself to organs and would not have come out. The surgeon told us that out of the twelve nodes around the tumour that they took out, eleven were cancerous. But he felt getting them out enabled the next stage of treatment to be successful. Kevin now has to recover from the operation, and we will then see a consultant to discuss further treatment. We both feel, again, that everything will be OK now, although we realise there is further treatment ahead.

Due to the operation, Kevin now has a stoma, but after over thirty years with a catheter, it's just another challenge to deal with, get used to, and he will—we will. Kevin spent just over a week in hospital, leaving on Monday 23 April. It was so, so good to have him home, so good.

Friday, 27 April

We went to Whiston Hospital to see the surgical consultant, Mr A, and some members of his team and the cancer team including the colorectal clinical nurse specialist (CCNS). The inference is the cancer may have spread locally, but there is no evidence it has spread to Kevin's chest and lungs, which is good news. Mr A was also pleased that Kevin's stomach wound had healed really well and that Kevin felt well. We are now awaiting appointments to see the cancer consultant regarding further treatment, which could mean going Christie Hospital in Manchester for an operation to put a chemo hot liquid (one-off hit) inside the stomach. Or we may need to go to a hospital in Merseyside for chemotherapy, intravenous or tablet form. A lot to take in, but positivity is the only way forward.

Saturday, 12 May

Received a letter to see Dr K, cancer consultant, on Thursday, 17 May.

Wednesday, 16 May

The CCNS from Dr K's team phoned to confirm appointment with Dr K. The CCNS said Christie Hospital have recommended chemotherapy, as opposed to the hot-liquid chemo treatment because eleven of the twelve nodes removed were cancerous. But a scan was needed to confirm the exact treatment plan. If the plan was for intravenous chemo, a three-month session would commence six weeks after the operation.

Thursday, 17 May 2018

We had the appointment with Dr K, and he told us:

- It is an aggressive cancer, stage 4. They can see this by the deformed cells. Two to five years life expectancy. I don't know how I'm even typing this; we are not accepting that—not).

- Of twelve lymph nodes removed, eleven were cancerous.

- One side margin could have cancer cells, but they are microscopic and cannot be seen by the human eye.

- Chemo intravenous treatment will begin 7 June. This is approximately four to six weeks after his operation because Kevin needs to be strong for chemo.

- There will be six sessions, so lasting three months—June, July, August (two per month)—at St Helens hospital, Lilac Centre (the cancer unit). He will take a nine-day course of chemo tablets between treatments.

- A scan will be done before the first chemo. Just before 7 June. It cannot be done before then because the inside stomach area needs to be completely healed from the operation to enable a clear view.

- If the scan shows cancer in the peritoneum (membrane lining), Kevin may be referred for hot-liquid zhemo treatment and/or any organ removal at Christie Hospital as it specialises in the membrane area.

- Intravenous chemo is a two-hour drip session but may take longer at some sessions.

- After chemo treatment Kevin is to return for check-up/scan.

Friday, 18 May

The CCNS phoned us to arrange a weigh-in Monday, 21 May, at Whiston Hospital on ward 4C, the hoist weigh facility. Kevin is dreading this; they are so difficult for him to get on and off of because of his paraplegia.

All chemo patients have to be weighed prior to chemotherapy in order to get the dosage right.

Monday, 21 May

Weight: 14.5 stone (91.5k), at Whiston, ward 4C with the CCNS. Weigh process was difficult for him. Kevin said never again! Next time we will find a hospital with a weigh bridge, such as Southport SI unit. It's sad and distressing that general hospitals don't cater for paraplegics in this type of instance.

Then we took the No. 10 bus to Liverpool town to spend Miller & Carter restaurant vouchers and have drinks with sis Janet and Alan at sunny Albert Dock. We ran out of the hospital, well we wheeled and ran. (jeepers that no. 10 bus seems to stop all over the place, took ages – as my dad used to say you need a packed lunch on such a journey)

Freedom to live. That's what life is about. Grab what you can when you can.

June 2018: Macmillan Finances

We first saw Macmillan at home prior to chemo in June 2018. Generally, there is no help available to us apart from Carers Allowance, which in January 2019, I decided to apply for. I am the chief cook and bottle washer, food shopper, ironing maid, gardener, errand-runner, electrician, plumber, carpenter, decorator, dog walker, bin mover, car washer, super-king-size duvet changer, etc., etc., etc. We have both worked and paid into the system. Now we need a bit of financial help, so I can spend time with Kevin.

Friday, 1 June

Booked patient transport, the first of many. The week before each chemo treatment we would book transport and arrange bloods. Kevin needs to have his bloods checked before each chemo treatment.

Tuesday, 5 June

Kevin had a computerized tomography (CT) scan at St Helens Hospital, and pre-chemo assessment at the Lilac Centre (the cancer chemo treatment centre within St Helens Hospital). This was with a department cancer nurse, a lovely woman, who made us feel as relaxed as we could be, and who answered all our questions and concerns. Quite scary though; she had to inform us of the worst-case reactions, symptoms. We had a tour of the centre to familiarise ourselves with the place in readiness for the first chemo treatment there. They do prepare you…. Well sort of.

Thursday, 7 June 2018: First Round of Chemo, First Session

The patient taxi transport arrived at 9 a.m. for the 10 a.m. session. Scary first day, but everyone looked OK in the waiting room, except one really noisy woman. This woman had two friends with her, and they talked constantly. And as it was our first session, it was quite unnerving. We found it difficult to listen to the nurse about what the procedure would be and the tablet information she was trying to explain to us. Also, there was a volunteer offering tea, coffee, and sandwiches. The volunteer was a nice person but a bit over the top with the comical sense of humour. That can be stressful. Well, it was to us, but it may help others.

'Hooked up' (intravenous chemo drip needle into Kevin's hand) by 11.45, finished at 1.45pm. This was followed by a fluid flush into the drip to clear out any chemo mixture residue. Given first lot of tablets—three days of steroids and nine days of chemo tablets. Also anti-nausea and diarrhoea tablets.

Waited an hour for transport home. Arrived home about 4 p.m. It was a long, long day.

Symptoms after this session: a raspy, soft voice.

Kevin started a schedule of filling his weekly tablet box and taking and recording his temperature every day during chemotherapy. This is mandatory. Kevin is very organised. Love him so much.☺

Friday, 15 June 2018

I booked patient transport and phoned the district nurse to confirm visit to our home to take bloods for the chemo session on 21 June.

Thursday, 21 June 2018: Second Chemo Session, 10 A.M.

Patient transport ambulance arrived at 9 a.m. Had bit of trouble strapping wheelchair into it but two very nice crew to help. Arrived at hospital at 9.30 a.m.

Taken to start treatment at 10 a.m. Trouble finding vein today; Kevin's hands were cold, so between 10 and 11.30 a.m., tried left hand three times, right hand once, and left arm once. They put warm packs on his hand to try to warm him up. Three nurses and five tries to get needle into a vein. Eventually succeeded on the sixth try with left hand. It's so heart-breaking to see Kevin going through this. More than words can describe.☹

It was very busy in there today. Tablets 'to go'—three days of steroids and nine days of chemo tablets. Also anti-nausea and diarrhoea tablets.

Kevin had three hours of chemo because it was in a small vein, 11.30 to 2.30pm. Then a fifteen-minute flush. When finished, Kevin's fingers were stiff, and he could not move them on his left hand for hours. Return patient transport turned up at 1.30 but had to go away as Kevin was not ready. I phoned patient transport at 3pm to collect us. There seemed to be a mix up in collecting us. Because they had been here earlier, the job was signed off as done. But we hadn't gone home! Finally home at 4.35pm. Along, long day again. But Tommy (brother) went to our home during the day to let the dogs out in the garden for us.

Symptoms after this session: raspy, soft voice; tingly, stiff fingers; and sore jaw when eating cold things.

29 June

Booked patient transport and confirmed district nurse for visit to take bloods.

Thursday, 5 July 2018: Third Chemo Session, 10 A.M.

Patient transport arrived at 9 a.m. Ambulance again.

Quieter at Lilac Centre this time, and Kevin went prepared, with fleece and gloves on. We had heating on at home before transport arrived to keep him and his hand warm! And lots of warm drinks.

Started treatment at 10.30. Left hand—needle in on the first attempt. Yay! Two hours of chemo. We both enjoyed a cappuccino and caramel bar to celebrate. Tablets to go: three days of steroids, and nine days of chemo tablets. Also anti-nausea and diarrhoea tablets. Flushed and finished about 1 p.m.

Then we had to meet with the nurse practitioner (NP). This is normal after three sessions of chemo to see how things are going. We queried the scan as we thought Kevin was to have one halfway through, but she said it is at the end. The NP told us that Kevin's bloods were very good, i.e., 3 (any number –14 is a good rate), showing no signs of active cancer. Positive news.☺

Return ambulance picked us up at 2 p.m., and we arrived home at about 2.30.

Symptoms after this session: raspy, soft voice; tingly fingers; odd feeling in jaw when eating cold food or drinking cold drinks. More tired this time. Also a loss of strength in shoulder when lifting himself from chair onto bed.

After this session, we got the train to Birmingham NEC to the Motability Roadshow. We thought it was the best place to view lots of different cars under one roof, so to speak. It was tiring for Kevin, but well done him as we got some ideas about the new car and adaptations for him. I know this sounds like a silly thing to do, but Kevin needed a car, and it seemed like we were doing a normal thing, a positive step going forward.

13 July 2018

Booked patient transport and confirmed district nurse for visit to take bloods.

Thursday, 19 July 2018: Fourth Chemo Session, 10 A.M.

Patient transport arrived at 9 a.m. It was a taxi with a nice, helpful driver.

Bit of a wait for treatment to start. Kevin worried about his hand getting cold, and I was stressed about Kevin worrying. Started at 11 a.m. to put needle in. Second try needle in at 1130 a.m. But then the flush buzzer went off. Waited thirty minutes to start chemo after that, hence 12.30 start, two and a half hours after we had arrived. Nurse said bloods OK, but calcium up. Apparently, it was a bit low last time, but we don't remember them telling us that. Again, treatment area very busy; lots of chemo patients today.

We always seem to have difficulty with wheelchair placement in the treatment area. There is not much room to put another chair for me to sit on, next to Kevin. Normally the cancer patient would sit in a comfy relaxer chair, but we always had to move these, thus reducing the room for Kevin's wheelchair and a chair for me. Something someone not in a wheelchair would not have to deal with. I got stressed over this. I just wanted to sit by Kevin, and for Kevin to have some space from others whilst going through his treatment.

Kevin did not need nausea or diarrhoea tablets today to take home, just usual chemo and steroid tablets. Finished at 2.55, taxi at 3.30, home at 4.00pm. A long day, and we are tired. With regard to latter, it's not so much the hours, It's what goes on during those hours and the stress of the situation that makes you tired. Tablets to go: three days of steroids, and nine days of chemo tablets.

Symptoms after this session: raspy, soft voice; tingly fingers; odd feeling in jaw when eating cold food or having cold drinks. Again, loss of strength in arms. This impacts so much on lifting himself on and off his wheelchair.

27 July 2018

Arranged two patient transports for the first and second of August—consultant appointment and chemo treatment on separate days.

Tuesday, 31 July 2018

District nurse to home to take bloods.

Wednesday, 1 August 2018, 10 A.M.

Appointment with Mr A, surgical consultant, at the St Helens Urology Centre.

Did not see Mr A but saw a doctor from his surgical team. This sometimes happens, and it is absolutely fine. They are all lovely, supportive people. We were told Kevin's liver, kidneys, and colon are all functioning well. The doctor was pleased with Kevin and thought he had put on weight. The doctor queried if Kevin had any stomach pains or problems. Kevin said he had none. Scan will be done at the end of chemo. The multidisciplinary team (MDT) will review the scan results and then decide what further treatment is necessary.

As we were leaving, Mr A saw us in the corridor and tapped Kevin on shoulder and said he was pleased with his progress and how he looked. Mr A is so nice. It's comforting that he is Kevin's consultant.

Patient return transport arranged. The door fell off the ambulance as we got to St Helens this morning, so we were not sure if an ambulance or patient taxi would be our way home. Return transport OK for ambulance. Door was fixed and all good.

Thursday, 2 August 2018: Fifth Session, 11 A.M.

Transport picked us up at 10 a.m., and we arrived at 10.15 at St Helens for Kevin's next-to-last session. We were told they were running behind time and gave us vouchers for a cup of tea. We sat in cafeteria with a beeper until 10.45, went back to Lilac Centre, and sat for another thirty-five minutes until we went in at 11.20 a.m when we were called to start treatment. A trainee who was trying to put the needle in Kevin's hand had trouble finding a vein, trying twice. Another nurse tried twice and then another. The last one successfully 'stabbed' Kevin after five tries. (Kevin said his veins hide.☺). Chemo started at 12.15. About 1.15 p.m., the treatment machine attached to the guy next to Kevin bleeped, and Kevin's treatment machine was nearly switched off by mistake! Chemo finished at 2.15. After the flush, we left the centre at 3 p.m. Waited about thirty minutes for patient transport, arriving home about 4 p.m.

Also, today the nurse thought Kevin's bloods showed a problem with pancreatitis. This delayed chemo as they had to check it out. Everything was OK, but it was another stressful and worrying day.

Kevin felt tired and stressed.☹

Tablets to go: three days of steroids and nine days of chemo tablets.

Symptoms after this session: raspy, soft voice; tingly fingers; odd feeling in jaw when eating cold food or drinking cold drinks. Again, loss of strength in arms which is not so much of a problem for a 'walking' person, as we call non-paras, but a huge thing for Kevin to deal with.

Friday, 10 August 2018

We were so busy looking at cars online from a shortlist we liked at the NEC, I forgot to book for patient transport! Normal life took over from cancer life for one nano of a second.

Monday, 13 August 2018

Phoned for patient transport for last chemo on 16 August, 11 a.m. but will book for 10.30 a.m. to save waiting around so much as Kevin gets cold and stressed and his veins disappear. Also phoned to confirm district nurse, for Tuesday, 14 August for bloods.

Thursday, 16 August 2018: Sixth and Final Chemo Session, 11 A.M.

Transport taxi arrived at 10.30. Arrived St Helens Lilac Centre at 11 a.m.

Prior to leaving had heating on at home. And as usual, Kevin wore his fleece and gloves all the time to keep his hands warm!

The nurse took us through to be hooked up at 11.15. And then we waited. At 11.40 the nurse came back to say there seemed to be an anomaly with the blood test results regarding the kidney function. The nurse had to check with the NP to see if chemo treatment could go ahead today because of this. The NP had passed us as we entered the ward for chemo at 11. 15, but she was now out at the X-ray dept. At noon the nurse came back to say she had spoken with the NP, and it was OK to start treatment. The nurse also said the blood results showed his kidneys were functioning well.

First needle in was a success at 12.10, but the vein was thin. So two and a half hours of chemo, then flush. We finished about 3 p.m. Transport came at 3.30 p.m., and we were home by 4 p.m. A long, stressful day, especially with the blood test anomaly and wait to start chemo.

The usual tablets to go: three days of steroids, and nine days of chemo tablets.

Symptoms after this session: raspy, soft voice; tingly fingers; more tired than usual; lack of strength for getting on and off bed; a bit forgetful; a bit down.

Friday, 17 August 2018

Received appointment letter to see Dr K, cancer consultant, on Monday, 10 September 2018 at 10.15, at St Helens Hospital.

Received letter to see Mr A, surgical consultant, on 3 October 2018.

Monday, 3 September 2018

Scan done.

Monday, 10 September 2018: Scary Day

Transport was late. We were late, oh my, oh my. Dr K was not at the Lilac Centre. Rushed upstairs—well, rushing to lifts to get to the red zone. Not there either. Back down to ground floor red zone. Found him!

We were both on tenterhooks as we entered the room for the results. Dr K, smiling, said there was no measurable cancer found on scan. He was very happy about that and with how Kevin coped with chemo over last three months. OMG, we are both in a bit of a la-la land state. Dr K will send the scan to Christie Hospital in Manchester to see if they want to do a more in-depth scan, and we will hear via letter either way

Kevin mentioned he had some issues since coming off the chemo, such as, a toothache, deafness in his right ear, upset stomach, and lack of taste. Dr K did not seem concerned.

Dr K does not want to see Kevin for another three months—10 December 2018, 9.45 a.m., at St Helens. Christie specialises in the stomach-lining area, but even if there is some cancer there, it is small as the main scan does not show any.

We went for a coffee and had to take it all in. We busily texted family and friends the good news. The taxi transport home was looking for us; we are normally looking for them!

No measurable cancer. ☺☺☺

From feeling stressed, exhausted to relaxed, exhausted. It's like being in a fog for the last five months, and now we can see the blue sky.

It's a roller coaster of feeling sick in the pit of your stomach, with waves of sadness, anxiety, and positivity thrown into the mix.

I will ring in two weeks, around 24 September, regarding any further development from Christie. Dr K will send the results to Christie and other consultants.

17 September 2018

The CCNS phoned us to say he is arranging an appointment at the Royal Liverpool Hospital for a positron emission tomography (PET) scan, which Christie had asked for.

10 October 2018

PET scan at Royal Liverpool Hospital, 12.30.

14 October 2018–15 March 2019

Between these dates, Kevin went through a bad phase of drinking; then he stopped. What was the trigger for drinking - sadness, depression – Cancer? Kevin is a realist, and maybe the news on 10 September was not enough to stop his fears.

Sunday, 14 October 2018

Kevin was very drunk and, 'Angry with cancer.' I went to bed at 7.30 p.m.

Thursday, 18 October 2018

I was at work from eight o'clock until five. I got home, took the dogs out, and cooked dinner. Kevin said he was watching *Gold Rush* tonight, so no TV option for me then! He had, had a drink, angry with cancer.

Tuesday, 23 October

Kevin had a drink. A large bottle of Bacardi was full on Saturday, 20 October, but is half-full today.☹

Thursday, 25 October

Kevin had a drink. And when I mentioned about a friend being depressed, Kevin said, 'What has he got to be depressed about? He is not dying.' ☹

I know what he means, I do. But I don't know how to answer him.

Friday, 26 October

I came home from work, and Kevin was happy. He had not been drinking. Phew! The journey home in the car from work had become a worry for me, wondering how Kevin had been all day and how he would be when I got home.

Monday, 29 October 2018

Kia Niro car delivery! The accompanying picture shows Kevin in the driver's seat. Happy day. But we did not know then that during and after Kevin's second round of chemo, he would become too weak to get in and out of the car.

7 November 2018

I came home from work at 6.30. Kevin has been drinking but is not drunk.

8 November 2018

I was at work 2 p.m. to 7.30 p.m. Kevin was watching a match when I got home, but he had been drinking. At 9 p.m. I told him to go to bed as he was flopping in his chair; I was worried he would fall out. But he wouldn't go to bed.

Friday, 16 November 2018

The CCNS phoned regarding the results of the PET scan. The results showed there are a few active lymph nodes behind the peritoneum; that is, outside the lining. Their location rules out the chemo treatment at Christie's, and they are no longer involved. ☹☹

We will see Dr K on 10 December to discuss further chemo treatment. The systemic option is more chemo, or if we wait a few months and then do another scan.

25 November 2018

Kevin did not drink. We slept all night; that is, there was no catheter bag change in the middle of the night.☺

Monday, 26 November 2018

When I got home from work, Kevin had been drinking. But he was OK.

4 December 2018

Kevin got an email from a work colleague about doing work in 2019. Kevin asked me, 'Will I be here?' Kevin hasn't told his colleague about the cancer.

Went shopping for some Christmas gifts. Kevin said, 'Don't buy for me!' Kevin responded to a Facebook post about a friend going to New York and how excited she was, Kevin said, 'Enjoy it while you can.' He didn't mean about the friend, just in general—enjoy while you can.

7 December 2018

Kevin drank a quarter bottle of Bacardi, and ate fish and chips at 8 p.m. His stoma bag burst in night. Bad night, bad night!☹

Sunday, 9 December

I made a roast chicken dinner. When I said we can have leftovers on Monday, Kevin said he, 'won't be back.' I made coffee, and Kevin said, "Last coffee before sentencing.' He is angry with cancer.

Later I was watching something on TV, and Kevin stormed off to do shredding. It was noisy for about ten minutes, and I couldn't hear TV.

Monday, 10 December 2018

I asked Kevin what he wanted for breakfast, and he said, 'Last supper', thinking they will keep him in.

Dr K, cancer consultant, explained the results of the PET scan done on the 10 October. The scan unfortunately demonstrated a PET avid para-aortic lymph node and some low-grade uptake in some of the peritoneal abnormalities. On that basis, as the CCNS had informed us in November, Christie's ruled out any possibility of local surgery. The CT scan will be repeated in January, prior to meeting with Dr K on 14 January.

Friday, 14 December 2018

I went to work, parked, and phoned our CCNS, asking for help, who we can talk to about Kevin's feelings. He suggested Macmillan helpline, but I was hoping there was someone we could talk to when we went to the hospital. I know Kevin would not talk to a helpline with me.☹

Got myself together and went into work, 10.30 to 7. Came home, and Kevin was drinking.

Friday, 21 December 2018

Elaine, Dean, Hayley, and Rae came over from noon until two. It was nice. I worked from 2 p.m. until 7.30. When I came home, Kevin had been drinking, but he was OK.

Sunday, 22 December 2018

I went out about 9 a.m. to Santa brekky with my sister Susan, nephew Ian, Leanne, and kids. It was lovely. Back home at 12.30. Kevin had been drinking.

Christmas Day 2018

Janet and Alan joined us for dinner. Tommy and Amanda popped in for lunchtime Christmas Day drink at St Basils. It was a nice day. ☺

New Year's Eve 2018

Had a lovely, fun evening at the local social club—St Basils—with Susan and Tommy.☺

2019

10 January 2019

I was at home the seventh, eighth, and ninth. I worked on 10 January, from 9 to 3 p.m. Came home and found Kevin drinking. Took dogs for a walk, got back at four o'clock. Kevin was in bed, until 5.30 p.m.

14 January 2019

Appointment with Dr K. Kevin needs another six sessions of chemo as cancer cells are still in his stomach. Some have spread via blood to outside his stomach area.☹

Chemo started again a week later, on Monday 21 January, and finished 1 April 2019.

Monday, 21 January: Second Round of Chemo, Session 1

It went OK. And it was great that we didn't have to wait for patient transport as we used our new Kia to go to the hospital. But Kevin was a bit weak after and found trying to lift himself over and into the car was a step too much. We will use passenger transport for future sessions. Kevin is not using the car now. I'm trying to acquire an assist arm, but I think with even that, he is dubious about using the car. So we cannot go out together in the car.

I conducted lots of research into an assist arm/handle which would enable Kevin to use the Niro again. It would be located on the door at an angle, for Kevin to grip in order to lift himself into the Niro. Emailed the company in December 2018 and did not hear. I emailed again in January, February 2019. The company replied, saying they were looking into making one and would contact us. I explained the urgency as Kevin could not use the car without one. I finally received a response at the end of February. The company that makes them said they were unable to fit one to the Niro. Marooned again!

Saturday, 22 January 2019

I went out for Janet's birthday meal at 3 p.m. and returned home by 8.30 p.m. When I got home, Kevin was drinking and swearing at Space Invaders game. It was distressing for me. I'm sad after a good day. I'm sad because Kevin is ill, and I don't know how to help him. Angry with cancer.

24 January 2019

I worked from 10 a.m. to 4 p.m. Came home, and Kevin has been drinking. All he ate today was ham and cheese. I left more substantial food, but he wasn't bothered, or I suppose that's all he wanted.

25 January 2019

Kevin got up in night and could not get back into the bed, due to the chemo. he has no strength in his arms to transfer from wheelchair to the bed - It was 4 a.m. I helped him back into the bed.

31 January 2019

I worked from 9.30 a.m. until 4 p.m. Came home and Kevin had been drinking, He is now asleep.

4 February 2019: Second Round of Chemo, Session 2

All went OK. During this session, we received news of a viewing on our bungalow in Ottershaw. It came to fruition, and they made an offer. But they have to sell, so we are still having viewers in the meantime. We said we would not accept other offers until end of February to give them chance to sell their home and buy ours. Stressful situation selling, but probably worse trying to sell and buy at the same time, so think this is a fair compromise.

Thursday, 7 February

Worked 11 a.m. until 6.30 p.m. Kevin drinking but OK. But he is tired.

Friday, 8 February 2019

Kevin up at 4 a.m. I heard him get up to empty stoma bag and then drifted off. At 5 a.m., Kevin is not in bed! Kevin is in the living room with a cuppa and a biscuit. Again, he couldn't lift himself back onto bed. Helped Kevin back into bed.

Kevin mostly now getting up about three or four o'clock every morning to empty stoma bag. That is OK as we both can then get back to sleep until about eight or sometimes nine in the morning, depending on what the day holds. Thankfully I'm not working at Heathrow Airport anymore with the alarm going off at 6.30 a.m.! Also, now I have carers allowance, I can reduce some hours.

Sunday, 10 February 2019

Went to Basils to watch Chelsea; they lost. Our Tommy is with us. Then I picked Amanda up to join us. We had a really good night, but I could see we needed to get home as Kevin is tired. Good night turns to bad night in feelings. How can I explain? On a high, things seem normal. Then night ends, and the quietness of the night then lends to feeling low.

Saturday, 16 February 2019

We had a really lovely visit from Ray and Catherine—fun, poker, good friends, good time. They came so far for just one night, but we had a fantastic time. It took it out of Kevin, though, and he had chemo on 18 February. But he would have been on tablets the weekend before, so no real good time to visit. We must live; we can't put life on hold for three months, I can't let him, and he loved it. Thank you, Ray and Catherine, even though you beat us at poker!☺

Miss all our friends from Ottershaw. Always think I'll ring one of them, but then think, *Oh, they will be busy.* I miss them. XXXX

Monday 18 February: Second Round of Chemo, Session 3

Sunday, 24 February 2019

Elaine was going to pop over for the Chelsea vs Man City match. It would be nice for Kevin to watch with his sister, but they had colds, so it was best not to come. Would be nice to see them soon. His mum and dad too. I know everyone is busy.

The offer made on 4ᵗʰ February, on our bungalow in Ottershaw was withdrawn, as the prospective buyers decided not to move.☹☹

4 March 2019: Second Round of Chemo, Session 4

It went OK. Good veins today!

Saturday, 9 March 2019

Susan and Tommy came over for dinner. It was a really good, fun time. Again, you feel on a high, enjoying the evening. Then they go, and you feel deflated. That happened the other week. Life doesn't run smooth; it's a roller coaster of ups and downs.

I've been thinking about, *What is life?* Life used to be getting up for work, breakfast for us both, feeding the dogs, shower, dress, get on M25 at rush hour and sit for forty-five minutes going just three junctions. Kevin wheeling down to the office—a small bedroom at home–working all day, stopping for lunch at 1 p.m. Home from work, doing dinner, walking the dogs, and sitting down later in the evening to watch TV together. Then we'd do it all over again next day. Sounds boring when you write it, but believe me, now I know it's not!

When I was not at work, I would volunteer to walk dogs at the RSPCA rescue centre a few hours a couple days a week. Then at home, cleaning, shopping, gardening, and so on. Lunch was at 1 p.m., and we'd catch up with the news for both of us for just 20 minutes. We spent weekends seeing friends at a local social club or Miller's restaurant. Life ran as maybe life should. But over the last year, and now, I question what life is. It makes me think of Monty Python's *The Meaning of Life*. I think until you are living with cancer or some other life-changing, life-threatening situation, life is life, no questions asked.

Kevin shouts, 'Are you there?' Yes, I'm always here, sweetheart, because I love you.

Occupational Therapy (OT) and Ramp: Why We Needed OT

Our bed is now too high for Kevin to get onto because he has no strength in his arms to transfer himself to the bed. I took the castor wheels off - it is a SKS (super king size) bed - to lower it so Kevin can get onto the bed easier. That was no mean feat as it is a heavy bed! Looked in the garage for a jack, thinking I could winch each corner up to do this. It was a tyre pump, not a jack - I feel like crying. Right, need to gather some Herculean strength: Where there is a will, there is a way. I wedged the bed up with a ream of paper, so I could pull off the castor wheels. OK, I got the corner castors off with pliers. Job done? Nooo. There are middle castors- need more paper!

Kevin said ten times better, 'Champagne for everyone!' Well almost. I also put wood shelves on the floor to raise the floor level slightly. And that, with the wheels off the bed, did help. Kevin queried if the shelves would move. Move where? I had the shelves wedged between the bed's base and the built-in wardrobe!

It wasn't ideal. Macmillan put me in touch with an OT department to see if they could provide some sort of a ramp with a platform flat area. Put next to our bed, Kevin could wheel up the ramp, park on the flat area, and transfer from wheelchair onto our bed. I phoned them and left a message explaining our dilemma.

I left another message for the OT to see if they could source a ramp. Did not hear from them.

Phoned OT again. They are looking into it. I suppose they are used to dealing with adaptions/assistance aids for people with cancer, but not people with cancer and a paraplegic, so our request is unusual for them.

It's now been about five weeks since I first spoke to OT. It's a struggle for Kevin to get onto our bed, even with the makeshift raised wood. It has gotten so bad I measured for a piece of flat wood to go on top of the wood shelves on the floor to give a bit more height. We measured what we needed, and off I went to B&Q. Nice salespeople helped me with two large pieces of wood that needed cutting and then helped put into the car, which was a bit of a struggle as the wood was the full width of the car! I drove home with the boot closed by some string, praying I didn't lose any wood on the M57! Got home, got it out of car—just call me wonder woman, tee hee—placed it down by side of bed, and things seem better. Not great, but better.

After a visit from OT—without the carpenter who was going to make a ramp for us—the carpenter makes bespoke items for people with cancer who need mobility aids that are not 'off the shelf'. He was supposed to join OT to look at what we need (he had wrong date). Anyway, we explained the situation and we may now soon have delivery of a ramp. Watch this space!

12 March 2019: Ramp Delivery

'Right, then', as our good German friend Erika used to say. Ramp was delivered. It looked the part, but Kevin was not sure about it. It took a lot of effort via phone-calls, emails, and so on to find this, but I think he now prefers the two flat pieces of wood I purchased from B&Q! The ramp is too high, and he can't get off the bed now. I put the castors back on the bed to raise the bed again. My back has been aching last few days; an SKS bed is not easy to manoeuvre.

I just felt so sorry for him, and useless to help. Again, this—getting on and off a bed—is not something a non-paraplegic would find difficult, but it was a huge strain for Kevin with his arms becoming weaker with the chemo.

Kevin took his first shower with the ramp by the bed. He would have to wheel onto it after his shower. The wheelchair was wet with being in the shower, so this caused sliding issues with the wheels, even with the brakes on. Kevin spent fifteen minutes or more trying to transfer from his wheelchair to get onto the bed. I tried to offer solutions; for example, placing a cushion behind his back and/or under his right fist to give Kevin that necessary height when he lifts off his right hand to transfer. I left him and went outside for some fresh air. I could feel the anxiety building in both of us. He eventually made it onto the bed but dreaded the next shower. Why is all this so difficult. Kevin has a stoma and finds it awkward to wear his joggers as he is always in a sitting position in his wheelchair. Again, not a problem for a non-paraplegics. So many challenges, so many.

15 March 2019

Kevin's drinking stopped.

16 March 2019

I suggested we go out to look at some areas where we would like to buy our new forever home. I just wanted us both to get out of the house, have a change of scenery. Kevin did not want to go out as it had been raining. He said the drive would be wet, and he would find it difficult transferring from the wheelchair into the car as the chair would slip on the wet.

Kevin stayed in his office during the afternoon. It's Saturday, and I feel like I'm on my own, I need a glass of wine to keep me company, but I know he will pull a face!

Saturday evening in, *Live at Apollo* on TV. Great! A good laugh is always a tonic. But then the lady comedian was talking about doing the show for her mum, who had died two weeks earlier of stage 4 bowel and stomach cancer. Not what we really tuned in to hear, but we understand her situation. We can't escape it, even while watching TV.

17 March 2019

Lazy Sunday. After a four-hour shift, I then walked dogs in the rain and cold, brrrr. All back now. Had a hot shower and a glass of Chardonnay. Me, Kevin, Layla, and Bess all cosy at home.

Monday, 18 March 2019: Second Round of Chemo, Session 5

I mentioned to Kevin about drinking more water as the nurse said that that would help them find veins. Kevin said he has things to do and can't just sit drinking water. I took the dogs out.

Got to hospital. Three stabs, third time lucky. I had to leave the treatment room after the second try. I was upset for Kevin. It is horrible, really horrible. I didn't want him to see me cry.

Nurse asks if there are any issues or symptoms. Kevin says all fine, failing to mention the negative mental symptoms. I feel we need someone to talk to. Also, he didn't mention his nose bleeds when he blows it.

Tuesday, 19 March 2019

Wow, wow, wow. We got another offer for The Haven. I can't stop grinning, but Kevin said no champagne until signed contracts, or at least survey done.

Tommy's birthday today, and I went to see him. Kevin was not well enough for them to come here. Amanda got a lovely LFC cake ☺.

Wednesday, 20 March 2019

Got the forms from the solicitor to complete the sale of our home. OMG, how many forests, and so much information needed! Sat down with Kevin, filled them in, did the copies of information required - teamwork. Busy day—ironing, dog walking, clean bedroom, wash and dry bedding, put that blooming SKS duvet back on. Talk about difficult. Surely someone on *Dragons' Den* could come up with an easy way to put an SKS duvet cover on.

Kevin scanned all the completed forms, so we can keep copies before sending them to the solicitor. I made us lovely white, soft bread, tinned salmon butties. Kevin loved them.♥

Feeling like a normal day today. I had a well-deserved wine early evening. Well the sun was out, and the girlies wanted to be in the garden. Couldn't coax Kevin out.

Then while we were watching the news, a woman was talking about stage 4 bowel cancer and visiting hospices to look at where to die. Kevin said, 'Not for me'. He is not dying. I won't have him talking about dying; we are living. I hate these programmes/news story. Yes, cancer is real, but we don't need to see it so much on TV!

Kevin, wheeling from living room to office, said his foot was slowing him down. And he was huffing. I think he is upset with the TV story.

I thought, *Please, Kevin, stop banging into doors with your wheelchair. Bang, crash.* Banging against furniture. I feel like screaming when he does this. I try to ignore it. I feel its triggered by some stuff he sees on news, like just now. So I tried to ignore it and took another sip of wine. Angry with cancer.

Life: Sometimes Kevin has that negative face, and everything he says is negative. It wears me down. I want my positive Kevin back.

Sometimes driving home from work, listening to music, I feel OK, normal, not sad. Other times I feel sad and start crying. I just do, but I stop crying before I get home.

Sunday, 31 March 2019: Mother's Day

Picked up Janet to bring her to our house, where Tommy would meet us to go to Thornton Crematorium; our lovely Mum passed away in 1988.

When we got back home, Kevin was in bed. Janet bought lovely bag of birthday pressies for him. Tommy arrived to take me and Janet to the crematorium. We then went on for a drink for mum, It was a nice afternoon with Tommy, Janet, Susan, and Ian.

Tommy drove me and Janet back. Kevin stayed in the bedroom. They came into the house to shout hello to Kevin and then left.

I cried. I didn't realise Kevin had gotten off the bed. He caught me crying in the living room. I thought he wouldn't see; I didn't want him to. He said something about family, and I retaliated by saying his family had only been there three or four times in nearly two years, and especially as he was sick. I felt sorry later that I had said this and told Kevin I was sorry.

Sunday was a bit strained after that. Again, I felt awful as he needs to concentrate on his chemo the next day. Things were better by evening. Cancer is stressful, but it won't break us. I won't let it.

Monday, 1 April 2019: Second Round of Chemo, Session 6

We ate Scouse (Liverpool stew) and hand warmers on the radiator ready for Kevin (Kevin needed warming inside and out). Got there about 1.45 p.m. There was a long wait as chemo deliveries from Clatterbridge were delayed, a knock-on effect of treatment. Kevin got hooked up at about 3.45 p.m. Needle in the first time, thank goodness, on the underside of the wrist, though. Horrible. There was a bruise there the next day. Finished about 6.15 p.m. but waited until 7.30 for transport. It wasn't their fault; there are not many patient transports on that time of night. Home about 8 p.m., a long day. More Scouse.

Wednesday, 3 April 2019

Yay, Kevin's birthday. There was cake, presents, and Indian meal, courtesy of M&S. Champagne to wash it all down, of course.☺☺☺

5 April 2019

More shower difficulties because of the combination of chemo and T4 paraplegia. It took twenty minutes for Kevin to get back on the bed after being in the shower. It was caused by a combination of lack of strength and the plastic sliding seat/cushion/wheels. He got there eventually. Again something someone going through chemo who can walk would not have to deal with. Very stressful. Had a glass of wine or two. Needed it.

Saturday, 6 April 2019

So, at work today, I was looking forward to spending time later with Kevin in the garden as it was a nice day. Had a glass of wine. Very nice. Opened another bottle, and Kevin pulls a face and said, 'You will be asleep before the end of the film.' I wasn't. Angry with cancer.

OK, I had a bottle of wine, cooked pizza, and we watched *Gogglebox*. Then I suggested watching *Billions* instead of a movie. Kevin said, 'Yes, before it's too late,' meaning I'd fall asleep. It's like there are tendencies of mental aggression, nasty, selfishness. It's a bad situation. It's horrible, and I just feel like getting out of the house, but I don't. Cancer affects your whole being.

Sunday, 7 April 2019

Cooker broke. Had lamb in and couldn't cook it! Went online to order a heating element and rescheduled dinner plans from cupboard tins—M&S mince and mushy peas.

Monday, 8 April 2019

Kevin's stoma bag is like a balloon. He said, 'Have to change it or won't sleep tonight.' This was midday, and he had put a new bag on this morning. I asked why he did not just empty it. He replied, 'You don't know.' Angry with cancer.

Left him to it, and then heard, 'Oohhh.' Ran to the bedroom, but it was nothing really. Just 'Oohhh.' I'm getting head pains again, but Kevin has cancer.

Walked the dogs and then went shopping. My back was killing me. Got home and mowed front garden as green bin collection is tomorrow. Then ironing.

Tuesday, 9 April 2019

Shower issues again. Another nightmare! Feel like crying. OK, I am crying now. Taking towels from bedroom for washing, and Kevin says, 'Sorry I'm dying'☹. No words. Sad, both sad.

Elaine had text us last week to say they would like to visit Sunday, 21 April. Great! I'll change my workday.

Wednesday, 17 April 2019

Elaine text that she is not well and may not see us this weekend. Also, if they did, would Saturday be OK as Dean was working Sunday. I'll swap back workday; Kevin likes me to be around for visits.

Easter Bank Holiday, 2019

Good Friday, 19 April 2019

It's Susan's birthday. I met family at Weatherspoons Pub, in Maghull, around 6 p.m. It was very nice. Kevin couldn't come.

Saturday, 20 April 2019

Elaine text to say they're going to Morecambe first. Arrived to us about 5 p.m. It was nice to see them. I told them to visit anytime. They left about 7.30 p.m.

Easter Sunday, 21 April 2019

After work I took Bess and went to see Grace and Jack. It was a lovely afternoon. Kevin couldn't come.

Easter Monday, 22 April 2019

Woke up looking forward to going out with Kevin for a drink, meal, and a show at the local theatre. Put it on Facebook as that made it real, normal. Left him in bed, and when I heard him stirring, I went to offer a cuppa. He is not in a great mood! Knocks the 'happy' stuffing out of me bit by bit, by bit, by bit. Deleted Facebook post. Felt sad. Told him he didn't have to go. I went out with dogs. I need to get out. I feel like crying or screaming but won't.

Tuesday, 23 April 2019

We eventually went out yesterday for a drink. But it was just too much of an effort and not enjoyable.

Wednesday, 24 April 2019

There was a problem in the night. Changed the whole bed at 4.30 a.m.

Thursday, 25 April 2019

Kevin got up to empty bag but found it very difficult to get off the bed. It disturbed the night for us both. Feeling sooooo tired.

Saturday, 27 April 2019

We had a lovely evening and dinner at home with Susan and Tommy. But maybe too late a night as Kevin was awake until 2 a.m., drinking water. Then he woke up as something had leaked again. Bed change.

Sunday, 28 April

I'm not home tonight. First night since forever not there. Hope Kevin is OK, but I'm looking forward to a full night's sleep.

Wednesday, 1 May 2019

The Fiat Doblo Dynamic wheelchair-accessible vehicle (WAV) arrived today. I was excited with anticipation. Well, until we woke up, and Kevin said why couldn't it be delivered in the afternoon, and he has neck ache!

I see this car as our freedom to get out together. Let's hope. Kevin is impressed with it. Great, he was. ☺

Thursday, 2 May 2019, D-Day: Results from Second Round of Chemo

Not good. Dr Gloom (Kevin's name for Dr K) said the treatment did not work. The cancer has increased in size, showing signs near the liver.

Trying another type of chemo starting 23 May.

We are both—what's the word I'm looking for—shocked, gobsmacked, unbelieving? All of them. Came home, we just feel numb.

As we came in through the door, Kevin said to Bess, 'You will outlive me.' Then I asked Kevin about the Chelsea match, and he said he hoped he makes it for that. He still has a sense of humour, but maybe underlying fear because … cancer.

Kevin went for lie down. I mowed garden. Stupid mower would not collect the grass, so I had to rake. Leg fell off Dolly the Sheep. Well, laughed really. Erika and I glued that leg on years ago at her house, and the sheep was given to me when she died. Then I cried round the side of house so as not to let Kevin hear me.

I ironed Kevin's three favourite polo shirts. Cooked chicken and had dinner. Needed a wine. Oh, and fed the dogs.

As we had a nice dinner, we talked about what Dr Gloom said. Kevin said, 'Let me talk.' His tone hurts; we both need to talk, and I don't deserve that tone. Angry with cancer.

Right. He is watching Chelsea on TV. I'm off to watch something and nothing in the bedroom.

Sunday, 5 May 2019

Going to Susan's for sue-beef dinner. Fiat car problem, but then it is OK. Phew. Kevin had an 'issue' with his meds effects, but we carried on to see them. We probably should have phoned and cancelled, but he was OK, and he enjoyed dinner. I enjoyed someone else making dinner for me.

Monday, 6 May

We went to Whiston A&E at 1 p.m. (bowel problem). I left at 1.30 a.m. on Tuesday, 7 May. Distressing long wait in A&E. I was so upset for Kevin. It's not fair; it's not fair. He has cancer, surely that meant they would not make Kevin wait in A&E for so long. Finally, he was taken to a ward. I had taken the car home earlier in the evening to feed the dogs and let them in garden. I was as quick as I could be, so to get back to him.

Tuesday, 7 May 2019

Colin and Margaret arrived. They were due to visit before this happened. I spent the next three days visiting Kevin in the hospital with them. They stayed in our Tommy's house; he stayed at Amanda's.

Wednesday, 8 May 2019

I received catastrophic, upsetting news. The house buyers pulled out, 2ⁿᵈ time this has happened to us. I couldn't tell Kevin while he was still in hospital. I tried to hold it together during the visit. Sue and Tommy came over in the evening. They took Margaret and Colin back to our Tommy's house for me. After they left, I cried so much I couldn't breathe. Gotta pull myself together. It's not the end of the world. well almost not.

Thursday, 9 May 2019

After visiting Kevin, I took Margaret and Colin to the station and then went back to Kevin. Came home. Put on pjs and cooked lamb chops. I fell asleep on sofa, so tired.

Friday, 10 May 2019

Kevin is coming home from hospital today.☺

I took the dogs out at 9.15 a.m. Kevin called, ready to come home. I said I'd be there between ten o'clock and eleven. He asked if I could come earlier, but I knew he had to get ready, and other stuff to do, so 10.30 should be fine.

Kevin is home.☺❤

Saturday, 11 May 2019

Kevin needed a plastic cover for his wheelchair cushion. He said he asked for it last night, and said I didn't remember because I was pissed. I wasn't!

He is still having trouble transferring off the wheelchair onto bed because his arms and shoulders are so weak.

Sunday, 12 May 2019

I'm really not looking forward to the next five days, working ten to six every day (covering annual leave), I'm exhausted, and I don't want to leave Kevin.

Going into work for an hour today to see Sharon and catch up on emails and information, before tomorrow. I am about ready to go, and Kevin needs me to hold his chair. How am I going to be at work next week?☹

Monday, 13 May 2019

'Day 1', as Kevin used to mimic the commentator on *Big Brother* with a brummy accent. Day 1 of a full week at work!

I told Kevin to stay in bed while I got up, showered, and walked the dogs. Kevin got up. I did breakfast for us both, and fed the dogs. I left Kevin a salad for lunch. When I phoned him about 1 p.m., all was OK.

I came home at 6.30 p.m, fed the dogs and made dinner. Kevin then went to bed as he was very cold although heating was on in the house. He also had a cough but only when he lay down.

I sat down at 8.30 p.m. and phoned Sam, out estate agent, about house viewings. I played with the dogs – trying to give them attention too.

I googled organic apricot kernels (and blenders). Our lovely friend Bernie said they help fight cancer.

Falling asleep on sofa, I awoke and went to bed at 10.30. But then I couldn't sleep, so I got up at midnight for hot milk and solitaire. I lay there listening to Kevin breathing, croaky. I worried about that.

Tuesday, 14 May 2019

Left lunch in fridge, all on bottom shelf, easy for Kevin to reach. Getting through week, busy, busy. Lots of *ping* (microwave) meals for Kevin. I was happy with some jam toast when I got home.

Friday, 17 May 2019

Made it!

Saturday, 18 May 2019

Up at 8.30 a.m. Kevin's stoma bag leaked and the dog (Which one?) pooed in living room. All clean by 11 a.m., and we had brekky.

Sunday, 19 May 2019

I suggested going to the Four Topped Oak (Ember inn, a three-minute drive away) for Sunday dinner. It would be nice after a busy week to have a roast put in front of me. Kevin was not sure. I know he doesn't like going out, but we went.

Monday, 20 May 2019

I couldn't sleep. I got up, had hot milk, and played solitaire until 4 a.m. Got up again at 8 a.m., left food for Kevin and dogs, and went to work. I walked Blackie on the way to work. I volunteer for the Cinnamon Trust, a charity that helps elderly people who can no longer walk their dogs. Sooo tired.

Tuesday, 21 May, 2019

Oh dear. Dog pooed again. My only day off, and I had to go to Tesco, Pets at home, and so on.

Needed wine in evening.

Thursday, 23 May 2019: Third Round of Chemo, Session 1

So, so glad we have the Doblo WAV. It takes a lot of stress out of the day knowing we have our own transport, so no more waiting for patient transport. Kevin said he is not looking forward to it. I know I wish it wasn't happening. Kevin was a bit miserable, but we got to hospital, and he was all OK and smiles with the nurses!

Bad start. Three tries at unsuccessfully stabbing into his hand, and another nurse—the head honcho—was called, who put the needle into the middle of Kevin's arm.

Home by 2.30 p.m. I put washing on the line, did the timesheets and expenses for work, fed the dogs, and made us Spag Bolognese - Kevin's favourite dish. Opened the wine. Need to source damp proof companies as the survey on Slade Road raised this problem, and we cannot put it back on market until it is done.

Friday, 24 May 2019

Left food ready for Kevin and the dogs. Oh, and flask of tea, which I was leaving all last week. He likes that.

Life: Not slept well last week, tired, then go to bed, then wide awake.

Sometimes, sometimes too often, I get that sad feeling in the pit of my stomach. Sad tentacles run through my body to fingers and toes, consuming me. Must be strong to resist it getting to my mind.

Both sisters are away on holidays. I wish, I wish, I wish.

I wanted to speak to Richard (Tricky) but just felt I couldn't as I felt sad. So I sent him a text message. I hope I didn't upset him. I feel on the edge, fragile.

Monday, 27 May 2019

I woke up with that horrible sad feeling again. I felt tired. I had pains in my right lung area, the top of my right leg, and my head. Just feel exhausted.

Then I sat down with a cuppa. I heard Kevin having trouble getting back on the bed, so I helped him.

Found out yesterday there is a surprise engagement party for Richard and Marcus - 20 July, I want so desperately to go, but I don't think I can. I can't leave Kevin now, even for one night.

It's been a bad day. I'm sooo tired. And Kevin is annoyed because he couldn't get Aston Villa v Derby on the PC. I told him to watch it on the main TV. I put it on and dozed on the sofa. Kevin never came into the living room, although he had gone through it to go to the kitchen and must have seen I had put it on. I shouted, 'It's on.' He came in. I dozed. Then the dogs needed to go out, pitter-patter on the kitchen floor. I need to get up and let them out. Just felt so tired I could cry. But I can't.

Made a springtime dinner with a new menu of chicken, asparagus, chives, and soft cheese. And I needed a wine, without the disapproving look.

I told Kevin Geoff and Sue are coming next Saturday. He was not happy. It had nothing to do with them. It's such an uphill battle to live life with cancer and all its side effects and not knowing how he will feel day by day.

Tuesday, 28 May 2019

Kevin was feeling really tired today. I didn't know what to do to help. Wish I could give him a bolt of energy, poor thing. Went out for an hour or so to meet up with Gill at The Griffin Pub, near where her son lives. She is up from London for a few days, so It was nice to catch up.

Wednesday, 29 May 2019

Kevin was still really tired.

Thursday, 30 May, 2019

Popped to see Ian and Leanne, Grace, Jack, and Cookie today. Lovely time. It was their ten-year wedding anniversary. It was really nice, and they asked us to go for tea anytime.

Saturday, 1 June 2019

Sue and Geoff arrived. We had a nice time. I just want Kevin to enjoy, have some normal time—for us both to have some normal time together.

Kevin was feeling well and not tired, and their visit gave us both a much-needed boost. We watched Liverpool win champions' league after a quick visit to Basils social club, on Saturday evening. Then our Janet joined us at home, which was lovely; it was great to see her. Took Sue and Geoff to Crosby Beach on Sunday for a doggy walk with Bess and Layla and then home for a roast beef dinner. They took us for lunch on Monday and then left for Ottershaw. It was a really, really good time.

Tuesday, 4 June 2019

Woke up with that horrible sad, sad feeling today. But we had a great time with Sue and Geoff. Maybe seeing them and spending a lovely time with them just added to the reality of the sadness. It feels like we are living because they were here, but then they were gone again.

Nurse came today for bloods, and it starts all over again this week. Chemo on Thursday.

We just decided to have a bacon barm for lunch. Yummy. Let's put oven on. Oh, and footage of President Donald Trump here for a state visit is very interesting on TV.

Wednesday, 5 June 2019

A new day. Kevin was himself again today, which is really, really nice. It felt like life is normal again. Is it? Our Tommy popped round.

Cronton Playhouse Theatre, a five-minute drive. I joined the email list of what's on. Got an email announcing *A Chorus Line.* Kevin said to go with Janet. He just meant it was not his thing, but I said, 'I want to go with you!' We never went.

Thursday, 6 June 2019: Third Round of Chemo, Session 2

It went well. Kevin is OK, but losing his voice. Having Doblo (WAV) for transport is such a relief; we are able to go, and return, when we are ready – no waiting around.

Friday, 7 June 2019

A bad night's sleep again. I lay awake until 2 a.m. Then I got up, had hot milk, and played solitaire. I went back to bed about 3 a.m. I had pains in my head again, and worry so much about what will Kevin do if I die, and what will happen to Bess and Layla. It plays really heavy on my mind. I hope it's a stress pain and not a brain tumour!

I'm so tired and, therefore, a bit narky. Kevin asked, 'Is Geoff going into Slade Road to take white wardrobes down before the damp-course company goes in on Monday?' 'Yes, of course. I've arranged that already,' I snap.☹

A good thing was that Kevin woke up and said he felt OK, and we should go out in car 'area hunting' today. That made me feel better, positive. Yes, he has mostly been like my old Kevin this week, and that's nice.

I rushed out to get the food shopping done to get back to go out for the afternoon. I meant to walk Blackie on way to Widnes, but I forgot. I didn't remember until I woke up Saturday morning! While I was out went to Specsavers and another optician's shop to see if they could fix Kevin's TV glasses - no joy. Parked in the wrong car park to go to Morrisons, so I had to walk, with the trolley, to other car park in heavy rain. I dropped the Jaffa cakes in a puddle. Exhausted, I started crying in car on way home. I needed to stop before I got home, but somehow it does feel good to cry, let it out.

We didn't go out this afternoon, too wet.

Saturday, 8 June 2019

I met Susan and went to the garden centre for tea, cake, and natter. Still having problems with my phone—the keypad is not showing—so I phoned Vodafone again! They told me to go to their shop, and if it needed to go away for repair, they would 80 per cent have a courtesy phone for me. I need my phone.

Sunday, 9 June 2019

Tommy picked me up to go to St Helens, the only Vodafone store in the area open on Sunday. They couldn't help and had no courtesy phone. They advised I go to Warrington Samsung, who could fix it on site. Went to Warrington—no Samsung in shopping centre, it was on a retail park nearby! Didn't have energy to go there. Tried Vodafone again in Warrington; they couldn't help. I wanted to get back home as going out 'area hunting'.

Got back, and Tommy had cuppa, and left. We went out to check out the village of Moore, just outside of Warrington. But totally nothing there for us—that is, ie a pub—so Moore is 'no more'. It's too isolated!

Monday, 10 June 2019

I went to work. Text Kevin, and all was OK. Got home about 5.30 p.m. Kevin was in bed - very tired - until about 7.30 p.m.

The steroids finished Sunday. Kevin talked about increasing the dosage as he feels it helps reduce his feelings of being tired and weak. Will speak to Lilac Centre at next chemo.

Tuesday, 11 June 2019

It seemed a good day. We went to Southport to register with SI (spinal injuries) hospital; they were very nice people. Went to Sparrowhawk Pub on the way back and had a really lovely meal, special time together. Got home about 3.30 p.m. Kevin went to bed until about 7.30 p.m. Poor thing, it did tire him out.

Wednesday, 12 June 2019

I'm going to Anfield (LFC tour) today. Our Tommy is picking me up at 1 p.m. Watch this space.

Anyway, our Tommy and I got there about 2 p.m. It was a fabulous tour. Wow, the history.

We went to the Arkles Pub. There was a life-size cardboard cut-out of Klopp standing there, as you walk into the pub – fun time. Tommy dropped me off at home. Kevin and I watched *Killing Eve*. Kevin's hair has started coming out.

Thursday, 13 June 2019

I couldn't go into work. I was worried about Kevin and couldn't put a face on for community support with what I'm worrying about.

Friday, 14 June 2019

I just walked the dogs. It was a really dull, wet day. I need to get ready for work soon, but I'm really tired. Clockwatched up until 4.30 a.m. I am worrying about selling Slade Road, among other things.

They didn't need me at work, so I came home. Washed Kevin's hair, and quite a bit came out. We're keeping cheerful about it. What else can we do?

Saturday, 15 June 2019

I dropped Tommy and Amanda off at Liverpool airport. They are off to Belfast.

Father's Day Weekend

Met Susan and Janet at the crematorium, and then went to The Grapes Pub. We had a nice few hours. Cheerio to dad. (Dad passed away in 2013.). Dropped in on Ian, Leanne, the kids, and Cookie.

Sunday, 16 June 2019

Decided I need to go down to Ottershaw to check if the damp course work has been completed OK. I haven't slept well this week; I'm seeing 2, 3, and 4 a.m. most nights. I am worried about the damp course on top of, well just life.

I left at 7 a.m. today. Back tomorrow, Monday. Quick turnaround but glad I did. Good job done.

It was really nice to go over to Marcus' house and see them, and Bob, and the lovely doggies. We had a nice roast beef dinner and then I went for a walk with Richard. Wish I had more time to sit and really talk.

Got back and went with Sue to Lesley and John's. It was very relaxing, helped by a few bottles of wine. All the bestest friends.

Monday, 17 June 2019

Sue and Lesley helped me clean around in Slade Road and do some weeding. The house is now presentable for viewers. Got back home to Kevin about 10 p.m.

Tuesday, 18 June 2019

I woke up feeling lost again. Shake it off, shake it off. Concentrate.

Wednesday, 19 June 2019

I covered a shift at work. I got home, and we went to St Helens to see Mr A; we saw a member of his team instead, nice chap. Just a surgical check on the stoma and so on. They thought Kevin had lost weight. Funny thing, as we were going to hospital, Kevin said his wedding ring is loose.

Thursday, 20 June 2019: Third Round of Chemo, Session 3

Saturday, 22 June 2019

I feel we are missing out on life. Runaways group on Ottershaw Club, and we would definitely be there with Trick. I want us to do those things again; I so do. We will.

There was a catheter leak at 5 a.m. I changed the bed and helped Kevin. We don't know why this Is happening. And we just noticed a lump at side of Kevin's stomach.

Sunday, 23 June 2019

I went to work at 10 a.m. Susan and Tommy came over at 4 p.m. We had a nice evening. On reading this back to myself, it sounds odd—bad day Saturday, 'good' day Sunday—but that was what life was. Each day could be different, and we took the good days and tried to enjoy them without worrying about the bad days.

Tuesday, 25 June 2019

Spoke to our friend Trish. Her birthday is today. It was nice to speak to her. I wish she was nearer; she lives down Plymouth.

Wednesday, 26 June 2019

The DN came today for a catheter change. Kevin was very, very tired, in bed most of the day. I went to see Susan, the kids, and Cookie. Got home, and Kevin was still in bed. He is extremely tired and feels sick. Life is not normal.

Thursday, 27 June 2019

Kevin is tired again, in bed and feeling sick. I gave him his tablets with a biscuit. I just want him to eat something, but he only ate the biscuit, some fruit, and an ice lolly until teatime. I told him he should eat something at lunch when taking the nausea tablet, but he says he can't eat because he feels sick. He is on the chemo tablets, which must be taken with food. I'd left breakfast stuff on table. It was still there at 3 p.m., when I got home from work.

Woke up 2 a.m., Kevin legs jumping - spasms. Couldn't then sleep, but Kevin got back to sleep, thank goodness. I made hot milk, played solitaire; saw clock at 3.30. Up at 7 a.m. for work. I don't want to wake Kevin in the night. He needs his sleep, so I creep around so as not to.

Friday, 28 June 2019

Gave Kevin tablets, biscuit, and drink in bed. Then he said he would get up and have shreddies, which is good to hear. But he is still feeling sick. I tried to encourage him to take the three nausea tablets with breakfast, lunch, and tea today. Walked dogs and went to work. I'm tired and a bit narky.

I did not go to see Grace (great-niece) in school summer fete, singing, as I got home at 3 p.m. but was tired after last night. Three days of Kevin feeling sick. Brekky still there on table again when I came in from work.

Made some food, but Kevin just picked at it; he is still feeling sick. We sat and watched France v USA. Kevin's head flopped in tiredness. I cried to myself without him knowing, and then got myself together; he can't see that. Not our usual Friday night. Went into garden with dogs, glass of wine, just crying in the garden. Can't phone anyone; they can't help. I listen to the song "Feeling Happy". How can you 'sing' those words, 'Cos I'm happy', and be crying your eyes out.

Life: Never take for granted what you think seem familiar, everyday chores/events - that is, work, housework, food shopping, gardening. Even the fun times spent with friends, out or at home are more special than you realise at the time; a lazy Sunday with a roast dinner and bottle of wine, and then back to Monday to start the same all over again. Never take anything for granted.

Saturday, 29 June 2019

Had BBQ. Kevin perked up slightly and ate the steak.☺

Life Challenge: April 2018 to June 2019

Kevin was harassed by a bank/debt-collecting agency who had him mixed up with a man with the same name and date of birth. Apparently, it is quite common. The harassment was in the form of telephone calls and letters, of which there were many. The messages left on our answering machine started with the debt-collecting agency saying they were a 'debt collecting agency'. How intrusive. It was for debts owed by the other Kevin Hughes. Long story short, *nightmare!* Felt like I was hitting my head against a brick wall trying to explain the mix-up to them. The bank blamed the debt-collecting agency, and the debt-collection agency blamed the bank for the error. They did not liaise with each other to resolve the matter.

During this time we also found out the justice system put three points on Kevin's clean driving licence. Those points also belonged to the other Kevin Hughes! Why, why, why was this happening during this time? The points really upset Kevin. He had never had any in all his years of driving. If he had not had to change his driving licence to a photo one, he would never have known as you don't check your DVLA online for no good reason – do you.

Monday, 1 July 2019

Came home from work, and Kevin is in bed. He got up, and we spent some time in the garden for fresh air. He was still feeling sick. He came in from the garden to rest.

Tuesday, 2 July 2019

Phoned the Llilac Centre because I'm scared, really scared, Kevin seems really ill. They advised us to go to A&E. Spent last few nights setting alarm to get up at 2 a.m. and 5 a.m., although most nights I'm awake then, to help Kevin empty bag while he was on the bed.

I knew he was too weak and he didn't have the energy to put his trousers on to go to A&E, and that's not like Kevin.

Got to A&E at 3 p.m., late in day because Kevin didn't want to go. We had to. It was another stressful experience. Got Kevin onto a holding ward about 11 p.m. Not sepsis, thank goodness. Stoma was empty, not working like it should. Just brown water in it for last five days.

Wednesday, 3 July

On Ward 1C. Kevin on all sorts of drips to replace all the 'body goodness' lost over last five to seven days. Test results showed no infection. Chemo nurse came to see us and said this is all chemo related. What does that mean? We came home at 5 p.m. and will go back for blood checks on Friday at St Helens Lilac Centre.

Thursday 4th July: Third Round of Chemo, Session 4

The session was postponed for two weeks as Kevin was ill and too weak.

Kevin said he was not hungry, but he needs to eat. What do I do? He had some breakfast and tablets and so on. He had to do his schedule, ie wash, get dressed, and I asked if I could help. He faffed, with no real response. I'm annoyed and hurt. I'm only trying to help but feel like I'm pestering him. Angry with cancer. Took dogs out and left him to it. Sometimes I just feel useless to help him.

Kevin's having trouble getting onto the bed. There are lots of huffs, and it's wearing on me. I got a bit annoyed and said I won't pester him. He needs to say when he wants help. I feel awful, but I'm really on the edge.

Text Janet to pick her up tomorrow afternoon. I need a drink! I know Kevin won't like anyone here, so I won't tell him until tomorrow. I know he just gets anxious. Angry with cancer.

Friday, 5 July 2019

Woke up 6.30 a.m. to a wet bed. Catheter bypassing again.

Up early to start procedure. Had breakfast and then noticed blood by catheter entry. Phoned DN at 8.30; she arrived just after 9. I changed the whole bed before she got here. I turned the huge SKS mattress around as Kevin thought it was soft on his side.

The DN said the catheter tube blocked with debris. He was not drinking enough. I added that he was not because he was worried about stoma bag filling up with brown water. Kevin got annoyed when the DN went to wash hands and asked what I said that for. It's the truth, but he said I'm making things up! Angry with cancer.

We went to St Helens, saw CCNS, and bloods were taken. We came home, I went to collect Janet. Got call from CCNS, saying Kevin is very low on potassium and needs a prescription. I went back to St Helens to collect it.

Had drinky night with Janet. Much needed. But she fell over, omg, and almost broke her nose!

Saturday, 6 July 2019

Kevin is feeling better today and not so tired. But there was another issue with the stoma at 6 a.m. Bed changed. Thank goodness for washing machines! Visit from Tommy and Amanda for a nice few hours.

Sunday, 7 July 2019

Went to work. Stopped at Tesco on way home for some stuff—water, Coke, cream soda, lemonade, and so on, phew, heavy shop. Kevin was tired when I got home and in bed, but he is OK. Got him his favourite—cream soda—and we had half a hot cross bun each.

Kevin slept while I made gammon, cheesy mash, and roasties. Kevin picked around the plate again. I felt myself stressing up. I don't mind what he eats, or doesn't, but please don't push it around the plate.

As we sat watching TV, it seemed Kevin needed to empty his stoma bag every hour.

Monday, 8 July 2019

Had to go back to St Helens for bloods check. We were there a few hours. Got home, and Kevin went straight to bed at 3.30 p.m. and did not get up rest of that day. Made homemade shepherd's pie and managed to persuade him to have some. Kevin's hiccups continuing; he woke up twice in the night with them.

Tuesday, 9 July 2019

I spoke to the LC. Going for tablets soon. Just walked the dogs. I need to mow the lawn and do ironing today. Kevin wanted shepherd's pie for breakfast, which is good, but not normal. I'm glad he is eating. He took a while to eat it.

Thursday, 11 July 2019

Up at 5 a.m. as stoma bag burst. I changed the bed and helped Kevin change the bag. Back to bed about 6.30 a.m. At least not up for work. Got up at 9.30 a.m. Both of us felt like we had got some sleep.

Reminded Kevin about his tablets. It's an effort for him to take them, but he has to. 'I've taken them,' he shouted. Not happy with that. I don't deserve that. Angry with cancer.

Saturday, 13 July 2019

Lovely visit from Dean, Elaine, and Gemma. But it makes me sad to hear of holidays, two, planned. No one's fault, it just makes me sad. What I wouldn't give to have even an overnight stay away to look forward to with Kevin. At the moment, Kevin won't even go out for a meal. I just feel exhausted with nothing to look forward to. I tell myself to snap out of it.

Sunday, 14 July 2019

Our Tommy came over to help trim bushes in front garden. Job well done. Hope not to be doing it much longer. We need to sell in Ottershaw to buy up north.

I had a dream. I was in a huge house with so much to do. Then the washing machine broke, and the sink became blocked. I walked along, crying. Someone asked, 'Are you OK?' I said yes and carried on. They asked it again. The next thing I knew, I felt a big, fluffy, long duster against one side of my body. It felt so soft and fluffy and comfortable. There was a scent on it that made me feel I was drifting into a relaxing sleep. And as I fell back, like floating, two people behind me, caught me.

The dream? It wasn't a fluffy duster. It was an angel with wings, and she alone caught me. I felt at peace. I did not feel any fear. I drifted into peace and tranquillity, and all my worries and stress dropped away. There was just peace.

Tuesday, 16 July 2019

The DN came for bloods. Kevin was tired; there was lots of huffing and puffing and bumping into door frames. I could scream, especially when the nurse arrived and Kevin was all hello and smiles. I know, I know. Life is the worst for him, and he needs to be how he feels.

I was going to suggest getting out in the car today for lunch or something but was wary as he was having bad day. Went to crematorium on my own, well with Layla, and stopped at Punchbowl for a small wine. It would have been nice sitting in sunny garden pub with Kevin.

Will I get down to Ottershaw for Tricky and Marcus's engagement party? I really hope so. I really need it and so want to celebrate with them.

Wednesday, 17 July 2019

Work today, all OK. And all OK at home. I might get down South this weekend. Kevin had a nosebleed during the night. I jumped out of bed in shock as Kevin shouted, 'Where is the blood coming from?'

Thursday, 18 July 2019: Third Round of Chemo, Session 4

The original 3rd session was postponed as Kevin was ill.

Spoke too soon! Up at 5 a.m. Bag burst, and now I am up and taking the dogs out. Then Blackie and then shopping. Might not get down south. Tired, I left the back door open at 5 a.m. when I let the dogs out didn't mean to, all safe & sound. Then I took a teaspoon out of the cutlery draw to eat my Frosties with. 'Won't get many on that,' Kevin said. "Just get a Frost.' ☺ There's my funny, hunk of happiness Kevin.♥

Chemo at 3.30 p.m. today. Kevin didn't tell the nurse about the nosebleed. Kevin was given different tablets, which I queried but Kevin just said, 'For God's sake.' So I asked him if he wanted a cuppa and left for about twenty minutes – I needed to. He smiled at the nurses and said he felt OK.

Saturday, 20 July 2019

Looks like all systems go for me to go down to Ottershaw. I've put together a large plastic box on the bed with a chair against it so it doesn't fall off the bed. It's full of towels, wet wipes, water bottles, black bags, bin bags, new bedsheets, stoma stuff, leg bags, night bags, and so on.

Started journey down South. Our Tommy drove, and our Susan came too. We had a lovely, lovely time. It was great to spend the few days with them too.

Monday, 22nd July 2019

Got home about 6 p.m. Kevin had been well. I did speak with him and text every day. Relieved it was all OK for him on his own.

Then … Got to bed and problems again with the catheter. All up at 4.10 a.m. to clean up the catheter leak, change the bed, and help Kevin. Back to bed at 5.30 a.m.

Tuesday, 23 July 2019

I woke up tired, with a sickly feeling in stomach, and pain in head again. I had not had any head pain since last Friday. Exhausted. I think we need to talk to someone. Kevin is ill, and it's really 'hard'. That's a silly word, an understatement, but it's difficult to explain.

Kevin is slouching on the table and huffing. I try not to cry again. I have the washing, tidying, and dog walking to do. Keep going.

Spoke to Trish, wish she could come to see us, but life is busy, and time just goes. You must feel like this when it's happening to you and your loved one, but you don't really see it when your friends are going through it, I realise that now.

You can't phone them at 4 a.m. You can't phone them when you are sitting on your own in the garden listening to 'Feeling Happy' while tears stream down your face.

I need to talk to Kevin about us seeing someone. He is ill. I'm trying to help, but more and more, I'm getting to the edge. I love him so much, and I don't want to take my frustration and stress out on him.

I caught poor Bess in the door today while closing it. I was trying to get her into the house because I was mowing the garden, and she throws the ball at me, and I walk backwards with the mower and nearly twist my ankle. She yelped; she only wants to play ball. Spool fell off the trimmer, which upset me. Hence shouting at Bess to get her in. Small things, massive upset.

Wednesday, 24 July 2019

Kevin was tired, but I suggested a little outing later for some fresh air. He said maybe. It's 2.30pm, and he has gone to bed. Just keep waiting for him to feel OK to go out. Waiting.

He got up about 6 p.m. I fed dogs and sat in garden and asked if he wanted to join me. He did. I had a glass of wine—just needed it. I'm so past caring now. The wine is my friend.

Kevin wanted spicy pizza. Great, so I ordered pizza. Kevin took one bite out of his and left it. I gave him half of my Hawaiian pizza. I think he thought he would be able to taste the spicy one, but he didn't like it.

Then I talked about buying a recliner chair for him for the living room - sod the cost. He agreed, and I was telling him about the fact they are bespoke and made to measure. I'd googled a company today while he was asleep. Made to measure, and they come out to fit, and so on. We had a plan.

Thursday, 25 July 2019

Saw the sun rise again this morning, up at 4.10 a.m., the bed wet, Kevin upset. That upsets me. It's horrible for him. I told him it's all OK, and sorted it out. Saw clock at 6 a.m. Must have drifted off then. Alarm went off at 7 a.m. Work today. Walked and fed the dogs before I left. Got meal ready for later and food ready for Kevin for the day.

Saturday, 27 July 2019

Kevin didn't want to take the last chemo tablets today. He is fed up of feeling weak with them. That's OK. He doesn't have to.

Sunday, 28 July 2019

Popped in to see Ian, Leanne, and the kids for an hour. Lovely visit.

Monday, 29 July 2019

Went for drive to Hale Village. We may live there; we both liked it. Kevin was in a better mood, and as of typing now, he still in good mood. Things are good.

Driving back, "My Guy" was on the radio. Love Kevin. He is my guy.♥

Booked Panoramic Restaurant for afternoon tea on Sunday, 4 August 2019, our seventeenth wedding anniversary. Traditional gift for a seventeenth wedding anniversary is furniture, so I bought Kevin a recliner chair in blue. In all our years at Slade Road, and Northern Lane, Kevin never used the sofa or chairs as it was too difficult for him to transfer from his wheelchair in and out of them. The recliner chair seat could be elevated up and down to match his wheelchair seat height, and then he could just slide across.☺.

Wednesday, 31 July 2019

Our Janet and Alan popped over today. Kevin was waiting for the DN so could not come out of bedroom, which was fine. He needed a catheter change. Then I sat in garden with Janet, as Alan had gone home. I was constantly checking our front door for the DN and left a note on the door to come in (front door opposite end of bungalow to garden). All OK. She came at 4.10 p.m. It was a stressful afternoon as I was trying to be there for Kevin and see my sis, juggling and trying to keep all parties happy, and live life!

Anyway, we came into house about 5.15. Janet said she was going in an hour. Kevin joined us and said, 'You're pissed.' We were not. Janet left about 5.45 in taxi. I cooked what I said I would cook—chicken stir fry and rice—so I am not pissed, but I'm upset. Angry with cancer.

Love him and certainly feed him.☺

Thursday, 1 August 2019: Third Round of Chemo, Session 5

Sunday, 4 August 2019

Our seventeenth wedding anniversary.

Had lovely afternoon at the Panoramic. Our Tommy and Amanda took us in the Dablo WAV so we could both have champagne. After our champagne afternoon tea, they collected us, we all went for one drink at The Britannia on the way home. They put cucumber in Kevin's Bacardi!. Made us all laugh. (Kevin likes his Bacardi as just Bacardi and coke – diet- no vegetation, tee hee)

7–9 August 2019

Kevin's mum and dad came to visit. I ran them back and forth to our Tommy's home (again he stayed at Amanda's, which was great). Lunch and dinners at Northern Lane. Kevin didn't want to go out, which was fine. Played cards, sat in garden. Special time.

Colin forgot I had said to just get one train - London to Liverpool, so he had put in travel search London to Hough Green, which took three trains to get here. Oops. Hence, to save them two train journeys on return, I took them to Runcorn for their return at 5 p.m. on the ninth, which meant one train back to London. No changes, no stairs, much better for them. I got home and mentioned what Margaret said about going out while they were here, and Kevin jumped on this, saying, 'No one understands I'm going through chemo!' Angry with cancer.

At this stage, I had to get out and went to our Tommy's. Didn't really watch the match as just needed to calm down in Dad's chair. ('Dads' chair was what Dad sat on in his flat, and is now in Tommy's conservatory – it is a comfort to sit in, like a hug)

Saturday, 10 August

Saturday was wet, so no chance of going out. Opened champagne, upmarket drink to my friend the wine!

Sunday, 11 August

Shall we go out? Kevin needed to get weighed at Southport SI Hospital. I wanted to drop stuff off to the kids for their holiday and pop to see Susan. No, didn't go.

Monday, 12 August

Long day at work. Busy and then manager nattering to me as I'm trying to write up notes and handover document. Left twenty minutes late. Came close to telling her to shut up! I wouldn't. Just the stress talking. Not her fault I needed to get home.

Got home. It's sunny. Kevin's tired, so I sat in garden with my friend the wine. What is to happen?

Tuesday, 13 August 2019

Last day for us to go out as I am working the rest of week. Mentioned it to Kevin in the morning. Waited until 3.30 p.m., but Kevin didn't want to go out. I felt deflated, like the stuffing knocked out of me, wearing me down. I walked past his office with my head down, and Kevin asked, 'What's up with you?' Do I really tell him? I can't, I can't. He is suffering with cancer.

Thursday, 15 August 2019: Third Round of Chemo, Session 6, final session.

Life only seems to have OK days, dark days, and in-between those are the numb days.

September 2019

Saw Dr K. Good news! The cancer has stabilised, so no treatment for three months. Scan and appointment in January 2020.☺☺☺☺

We can live a bit and have a normal life. So, I arranged a few things; friends from down south to visit, family over for a cocktail and quiz afternoon, family visit from Leeds. All is going goodish, and we enjoyed all this during late September and into October.

Then sadly, Kevin's mum found out she had terminal lower back cancer. From mid-October, Margaret has been in and out of St Georges Hospital. She is in pain, which they are trying to manage, and she is finding it hard to walk and go upstairs. Generally, Margaret is very down and negative about her situation. Unfortunately, she talks on the phone about both, saying things like, 'What's the point in more medication?' And to Kevin, "How long were you given?' I'm trying to keep Kevin positive and find it hard to deal with negativity. So now I'm trying to keep Kevin positive for him, and his mum.

October 2019

Sold our most lovely, beautiful home, The Haven, in Slade Road, Ottershaw. (I didn't write about the offer in late August. Scared!) Sad it's sold, but happy that now we can buy our own Forever Home, up north at last.

We started looking online more. I went to view a few, goodness all over the place! Viewed a bungalow in Watchyard Lane, Formby. No good, only two bedrooms.

Tuesday and Wednesday, 19–20 November 2019

I've been at work all day, and both days came home to Kevin having been drinking and upset. I know he is upset with his mum's cancer too; we both are. But how do I ask Margaret not to be negative? We have been trying to be positive about a cruel disease for the past eighteen months. Where there is life there is hope—that's our motto.

Saturday, 23 November 2019

Bad week but, went to see Tommy, Kate, and Ella today at Susan's. They were visiting from Beamish. So, so nice to see them.

Sunday, 24 November 2019

Kevin was in his chair, relaxing and watching TV, and then the chair seat was wet. Kevin got annoyed. Bloody cancer again. Tried to help but he refused. He is fed up with this bloody cancer.☹ Angry with cancer.

Monday, 25 November

Kevin is lying on the bed, whacking his leg to make it straighten down, spasms. I'm in the bedroom - just ask me to pull the pillow out from under it. The dogs are scared.

Went Christmas shopping in Liverpool. I needed to get out of the house. Met Janet and Tommy for drinks. It was a nice few hours, and then I went home.

Tuesday, 26 November 2019

Bed is wet again. Stayed off work so I could help Kevin get a shower, change the bed, and just be at home with him.

Called DN as the catheter is bypassing. DN advised us to go to A&E. She asked our local surgery doctor to admit us to GP assessment instead of waiting in A&E. Our doctor phoned us to say he could not get through, so we went to A&E and waited six hours. Not too bad based on past waits!

Dye scan required. Kevin finally got this on the Friday morning, three days after being admitted. Then it was the weekend, so nothing will happen; nothing happens in hospitals at the weekend. No plan, no communication. It was frustrating and stressful at Whiston hospital, and Kevin is fed up. Scan showed fluid between stomach and bowel, caused by cancer. Gastro team wanted to drain fluid. Cancer team said not to as fluid produces twice as fast when this procedure is done, and the area is then prone to infection.

Kevin was going to be discharged on Tuesday, 3 December. Then the ward doctor said he must stay to see the gastro team. Kevin has had enough, and after discussion with the ward doctor, we found out he did not have to stay. It seems like different teams are fighting over the patient; they each think they know best. It is horribly upsetting and stressful for the patient. Took Kevin home.

Wednesday, 4 December 2019

Woke up; the bed is wet. Problem again with catheter.

Thursday, 5 December 2019

Woke up, wet bed, ditto.

Spoke to a Macmillan nurse, Pauline. She is coming out to see us on Monday, 9 December. Seemed very nice, and she did offer to come out sooner.

Friday, 6 December 2019

Woke up, bed wet. To save Kevin's energy, I gave him a bed bath.

Off to work later.

Kevin still feels there is a blockage in his bowel which is causing the bypassing. We are awaiting a call from the pelvic nurse. Or is it the fluid pressing on the bladder? Appointment to see Dr K on Monday, 9 December, at St Helens Hospital.

Saturday, Sunday, and Monday, 7–9 December 2019

Ditto on waking up with the wet bed. We are both trying to keep our positive heads on and just get on with it until we see Dr K and try to get some answers.

Monday, 9 December 2019

Pauline, Macmillan, and colleague visited today. They are now going to help with communicating between the different teams. Thank goodness. I just didn't know where to turn to next.

Went to St Helens hospital and saw Dr K. Kevin and I are sad, disappointed, and frustrated with his lack of action. The catheter problem is not his area of expertise, so it is not his fault. It's the NHS system.

Dr K said the cancer has grown slightly, but he is not over worried. He agrees we need to get the urine issue sorted first. Dr K talked to us about the next steps in treatment. There is another chemo tablet that Kevin can try and a non-NHS trial tablet. The latter needs Kevin to be tested to see if he is compatible for the trial, and it is only a 3 per cent chance. If he is compatible, then a case to the pharmaceutical company needs to be made, literally begging them to let Kevin try it. (I would.)

Dr K could not fast-track us to a urology ward, but he made calls and sent emails. He phoned us at 6.30 p.m. to say he had managed to do that. (Thank you, Dr K.) We asked about going to Southport SCI, but apparently patient records are not transferable or able to be seen online, even if the NHS number is put in the system. What is this? It is 2020 next month! We both just thought the SI hospital would be more knowledgeable with the issues of a paraplegic, with cancer – we maybe clutching at straws.

Dr K suggested we phone the Lilac Centre to see if we could get a GP referral. Again, procedures, but we thought surely Dr K could do that? We are confused.☹ Anyway, after sitting and mulling this all over in the corridor, we left a message with Southport SI.

We then spoke to a Southport SI specialist nurse, who within fifteen minutes had a urologist phone us. It all seemed too confusing and stressful to try to go to a different hospital, so we didn't. We went home.

Tuesday, 10 December 2019

So we are in the hands of Dr K and Macmillan, trying to help us get to hospital when needed without the long, long wait at A&E.

Pauline, from Macmillan, phoned. They are having an MDT meeting at 11.30. They will discuss Kevin and let us know.

Then a nurse from urology at Whiston phoned. The nurse asked us to come in on Thursday 12 December. I said Kevin could not do another day like this, and we would have to go to A&E. It's not like he can jump in the shower each time this happens, like a 'walkie' person. The nurse then said to come to ward 4A at 2 p.m. today. Thank you.

Back home at 4 p.m., both feeling relieved. Saw a very knowledgeable doctor in the urology department who washed out the catheter and so on, and it seems to be working. Not holding our breath just yet, but we are hopeful we can now get on with Christmas and New Year.

Oh dear. Spoke too soon. At 11.30 p.m., the stoma was leaking., watery substance. It may be due to drinking more water. I helped Kevin. He was annoyed with it. He needs to take it calmer as it scares the dogs. Angry with cancer.

Wednesday, 11 December 2019

Different day, better day. We both cozied up in warm living room and watched *Daddy 2*, a Christmas movie. The 'bestest' afternoon.☺♥

Saturday, 14 December 2019

Well, dry mornings for three days, and then woke up this morning to hear Kevin saying, 'I'm fed up.' Half asleep, I asked, 'What, what?' and jumped up out of sleep. Kevin answered, 'Wet bed.'

Wednesday, 18 December 2019

Had to pop round to Tommy's for Christmas boxes—crockery, decorations. Life is … well not normal. Brrrr, dark and cold night. When I was getting ready to go, Kevin was on the bed groaning about stuff, quite loudly, so I asked, 'What's wrong?' I had offered to help; he told me to shut up. Angry with cancer, upsetting.☹

Thursday, 19 December 2019

Wet bed again, and Kevin crying, my heart breaks. This cancer is horrible, and that's an understatement. I hold and comfort him. We went back to Hot Clinic, Urology. We saw another doctor who thought the bladder problem may be due to pressure from ascites, the accumulation of fluid in the peritoneal cavity, causing abdominal swelling. Flush out again and went home.

Janet came round to help me decorate the tree. That was nice for a change. Had Scouse, made in the slow cooker, and then Tommy came round, too, for some Scouse. It was a nice evening, treasured times between other times.

Friday, 20 December 2019

I went to work, got home, and an appointment for the gastro clinic on Friday, 27 December was in the post. Thank goodness.

Saturday, 21 December 2019

Kevin was awake in the night retching. He feels he has something like fluid in his chest and was also sick with white/yellow fluid. Spoke to Macmillan. They suggested calling 111. We didn't, useless, and more stressful.

Wednesday, 25 December 2019: Christmas Day

Well, sort of got through Christmas. Kevin still off food but not feeling sick. He is improved from Sunday. So, Christmas Day was good; Kevin actually managed to eat some Christmas dinner.

I met our Tommy at the crematorium. Popped to see Ian, Leanne, and kids, and Susan and Tommy for a short time. Wanted to get back home to Kevin. Then it was just us, Bess, and Layla.☺☺

Thursday, 26 December 2019: Boxing Day

Kevin is still not well. In bed all day.☹

Friday, 27 December 2019

Had a visit from the bowel and bladder nurse, lovely lady. She will send some products but agreed it looked like the ascites was causing the bladder problems. The nurse told Kevin to drink more water and to use his catheter night bag for gravity. She said he is the expert on his catheter, so he should have known this.

Going for gastro scan this afternoon. Got appointment to see Dr F, the Macmillan doctor, on 9 January 2020. I feel happy, relieved with that as feel it is support for us at last.

Sunday, 29 December 2019

Kevin vomited green sick over the weekend and not eating or drinking. Called 111 early afternoon, and after much—too much—discussion on the phone a doctor on call came out at 7.30 p.m. Gave Kevin acid and antibiotic tablets. Useless, totally useless.

Tommy brought a couple of roast dinners on Sunday for us. 'All ask if you are OK.' Of course you say, 'We are OK', but you really want to say, 'No, not OK.' I've got a knot in my stomach. I feel sad and low.

Monday, 30 December 2019

I started with bad cold Saturday last. Got worse. I got up at 8 a.m. to let dogs out and went back to bed. Woke again at 1030 a.m. and asked Kevin if he had taken his tablets. He said he needs to eat before he takes them. I had, had enough and left to walk dogs, upset. Came back and gave him toast. I left the door open for the dogs and dozed on sofa. Woke up about 5 p.m., very cold.

Tuesday, 31 December 2019

It was a bad weekend. Kevin was in bed from Friday, 27 December. I've been to our doctor's surgery as Kevin is still no better. Trying to explain to receptionist was a nightmare! They asked, 'How ill is Kevin?' I tried not to swear at them; it is not their fault. Well the red tape is, I suppose!

Finally arranged for our surgery doctor, Dr K, to come to our home to see Kevin. Dr K arrived in the afternoon and prescribed more sickness tablets and Ensure vitamin drinks. The doctor told me to go to the chemist about 4 p.m. to collect them. I went and was told Ensure drinks were out of stock. He advised me to go to another chemist if they were needed. What, at 4.30 p.m. on New Year's Eve? I asked if they had any protein drinks similar to Ensure as I knew I had to get Kevin started on something as New Year's Day was tomorrow, nothing would be open, and he had to have forty-eight hours of tablets and drinks. After some checking in the chemist's they found four vanilla. Why the heck didn't they just give me them to me in the first place!

I was determined to have a wine or two, but that doesn't mix with night nurse medication over last few days, so I ended up in bed at 10 p.m. I've not done that on New Year's Eve since I was six! We both went to bed, but Kevin said he saw the new year in on TV, Big Ben with fireworks display.

2020

Wednesday, 1 January 2020

There was no change in Kevin all day. I'm trying to help him eat and drink something but no good. He was just sick. But it's not sick; it's a green fluid, well yellow as he had had two Ensure drinks last night/today.

Thursday, 2 January 2020: Hospital Admission

I phoned surgery at 9.01 a.m. and explained the whole situation, saying that Dr K had told me to phone and ask for a telephone call with him to check on Kevin.

By 12.30 p.m. there was still no call, so I phoned the surgery again. They said Dr K was out on his rounds and would call after 5 p.m. I knew, just knew, that was not good as Kevin was ill and needed to go to hospital. They phoned Dr K on his mobile, and he arrived at 4 p.m. Dr K said Kevin was to go to hospital, and he would write a referral to a ward rather than he having to wait in A&E. I dashed to the doctor's surgery to collect the referral letter. They could not get transport until tomorrow, Friday! No good. I was frantic by this stage. Kevin needed help; I needed to get him to hospital. Doctor's reception told me to phone 999. I went home from the surgery and phoned at 5.50 p.m. Although it was supposed to be a three-hour wait, thankfully they arrived at 6.30 p.m. We got to Whiston Hospital and to ward 1B at 7 p.m., but it was full! Sadly, we then had to go back down to A&E. Twenty hours later, Kevin got onto a ward (about 3 p.m. on 3 January). We were in A&E all night. Our Tommy went to sleep at ours to look after dogs. I had no car, so he picked me up from hospital about 6.30 a.m. I got home, showered, had cuppa, and went straight back in my car.

Friday, 3 January 2020

I returned to hospital between 7.30 and 8 a.m. About 9 a.m, I got in touch with Jackie from the colorectal cancer support team. I was reaching out to try to get Kevin out of A&E. Jackie came to see us in the A&E ward about 2 p.m. She got a doctor to examine Kevin, and he was then moved to ward 1C at 3 p.m. At 6 p.m. the ascites was drained. We were both relieved with the drain. The plan was to drain fluid, get back to normal, and continue with life and chemo tablet treatment in January.

The cancer journey is not straightforward. There are hopeful highs and hopeless lows.

I went home about 7.30 p.m. Kevin text me at 9 p.m. to say nurses were not emptying catheter/stoma bags. I got really upset and so worried that I went back to hospital at 9.45 p.m. I stayed for an hour. Bags were changed, so I went home again.

Saturday, 4 January 2020

After five litres of fluid were drained, Kevin felt no better. During the day he was sick, really sick. I mean a half to a pint of vomit, three times. Again, he's not eating or drinking. I was really worried. I asked about a fluid IV, thinking it would replace some of the fluid 'goodness' he lost. They said they would arrange one. Kevin needed a CT scan, but we were told he was not an urgent enough case to have one over the weekend, so it would be done on Monday. 'Not urgent'? Kevin has not eaten or drank much in last seven days, and he's spewing up a lot, and often. What's not urgent?

Sunday, 5 January 2020

I went into the hospital about 1.30 p.m. No IV fluid drip. I spoke to the weekend doctor, who said he had authorised one. I asked about the urgency of a CT scan taking into account Kevin's condition and again was told it would be Monday. So basically, Kevin just has to lie in bed for two days, not really eating or drinking, and being sick. Also, his catheter is in a bad state. I feel helpless.

I helped Kevin change his stoma bag today. I had brought in his electric toothbrush to give his teeth and mouth a fresh wash. I washed his legs and feet. They put on plastic boots on Friday afternoon, and they were still on today. They were making his legs sweat, so I took them off. I worry about the paraplegic situation. Do they really know how it's different for a paraplegic.

Very sad news this morning. Stephen died. We, Roz, and Stephen have been on the cancer journey together, both diagnosed April 2017—Kevin bowel, Stephen bladder cancer. RIP Stephen. I couldn't tell Kevin about Stephen while he was so ill himself.

Monday, 6 January 2020

Scan done. Hope to see Mr A, the surgical consultant, with Kevin for results. I don't know what time he does his ward rounds, but I'm in hospital from about 10 a.m. to around 9 p.m. I go home around three-ish for few hours to take care of the dogs and then back. Sometimes I don't have to go home as everyone is helping when they can.

Tuesday, 7 January 2020

Kevin was moved to ward 3B. A member of Mr A's team came to see Kevin. He said there is a bowel blockage, and Mr A will see Kevin to discuss what this means going forward. The nurse put a nose tube in—awful, awful. Kevin cried out in pain. After two days, we found out they put the wrong sticky tape on, and when it was changed, it pulled on the tube and again hurt Kevin!

Wednesday, 8 January 2020

Kevin was moved to Ward 4C, Mr A's ward. Mr A (surgical consultant) is a lovely man, trying everything he can to help Kevin. They said they cannot operate on the blockage. Macmillan spoke to us, but we are confused. They seem to be saying there is little time left. Awful week. Another scan on Friday.

Friday, 10 January 2020

Scan today, results Monday. The porter did not seem to know which type of scan Kevin was to have. I was trying to get hold of a nurse when the porter said no need, he *thought* he knew. I got upset and started crying. It's more important than just 'thinking' he knew which type of scan Kevin needs. This is my lovely Kevin they are messing with. The nurse had a word, and the porter apologised to me. He didn't know us and what was/is happening in our lives. It is not his fault.

I told Kevin about Stephen. He'd seen something about it on Facebook.

Monday 13 January 2020

Results of the scan do not show any blockage. Macmillan nurse said to try a bowel liquid that will find its way through the bowel. The next day, this procedure was stopped. When the MDT re-looked at the scans, they indeed saw a blockage, and this procedure could cause the bowel to rupture. Again, conflicting information, but perhaps all are trying their best.

More Macmillan visits. They keep trying different medications etc for two days at a time.

Kevin is now on a referral waiting list for Willowbrook Hospice. There is a chink of hope that they can help Kevin.

Had a nice visit from Tommy and Amanda last night and Susan and Tommy tonight. Ian came in on Tuesday. Everyone is very worried and just want to see Kevin.

Friday, 17 January 2020

I feel Kevin has deteriorated.☹☹☹

Saturday, 18 January 2020

I went into the hospital early this morning, and there was again, a delay with his IV saline drip. His mouth was dry, and they just said to sip water. But he can't as he feels full, bloated. I was dreading the weekend as less staff on and it seems there is no one to help. I came home and then went back to meet Elaine and Dean, who came to visit and watch the Chelsea v Newcastle match with Kevin. It was a nice visit.

Sunday, 19 January 2020

Janet came to sit with the dogs. I feel so awful leaving them alone so much, but I need to be with Kevin. Got home about 8 p.m. Tommy had brought around two roast beef dinners. Very, very nice. Janet stayed over, and I took her into hospital next day. She was pleased to see Kevin. Again, everyone is worried about him.

Monday, 20 January 2020

No news except that Kevin will have an ascites drain with a tap on it before he goes to the hospice. Dr T, a Macmillan doctor from the hospice, came to see Kevin. Dr T said the ascites drain would not delay Kevin going to hospice when there was a bed available.

Bad day after that though. The canula needed changing. Two tries, no good. A ward doctor needs to do this, so we waited from 5.30 p.m. When I left at 11 p.m., no one had turned up to do it. So the nurse put an IV drip through the butterfly tap. I'm so worried. Kevin needs the IV drip; his catheter bag was dry. I am so worried. Got in the car to drive home, and a Macmillan advert came on the radio: 'We are here to help.' Doesn't feel that way. I cry all the way home.

Tuesday, 21 January 2020

I went back to the hospital at 10 a.m., worried. The drain was supposed to be this morning. We are now told it won't be until afternoon. It needs to get done. Jackie, from the colorectal cancer support team, popped in. I couldn't help crying again. I just feel I'm on the edge.

Then at 1.30 they came to take Kevin for the drain. So I left the hospital and rushed to the shops for some bits - some clothes to give as a gift to Gemma for Grayson, and Hayley for Rae, as they are coming over at the weekend to see Kevin. Also bought more flavoured lip balms for Kevin. I got home about 3 p.m. and will go back to hospital around 6 p.m. In the meantime, I did the ironing and other bits, and spent time with the dogs. Sooooo tired.

Kevin text he was back on the ward at 3.40 p.m. All done, and he is OK. I will take the laptop back so we can watch Chelsea v Arsenal.

Wednesday, 22 January 2020

A few things happened today that were upsetting, so I need, really need, to get Kevin into the hospice. Whiston Hospital is good, but Kevin needs personal attention. It breaks my heart to see him not getting it. I pleaded with Emma, the hospice coordinator, to please not let Kevin spend another weekend here. The nursing staff are lovely at Whiston, but they do not have the time to give Kevin the attention he needs and deserves.

Thursday, 23 January 2020

Kevin got into Willowbrook Hospice. I am relieved he is there and in good hands.

Friday, 24 January 2020

Stephen Smith's funeral was today in Ottershaw. Our Tommy represented Kevin and me. RIP Stephen.♥

Saturday, 25 January 2020

Well, sitting peacefully in hospice with Kevin and got a phone call from Tricky. They are on their way up. Who are on the way up? Tricky, Marcus, Sue, Becci—all good friends.

Elaine had come over from Leeds, so I felt a bit awkward as it was her time with her brother. Hayley and Rae had brought Elaine over. It was lovely for us both to see them.

Anyway, after I'd gotten over the shock and stress—only because I wanted, needed to concentrate on spending all my time with Kevin—I realised it was the best thing. They are all special, and in hindsight, it was great for Kevin to see everyone, and they him. We left the hospice and went home to Northern Lane and had a drink, as Kevin would have done with us in normal times. They really did lift me up, so thank you, guys.

Sunday, 26 January 2020

Our Janet's birthday. The 'Ottershaw gang', except Becci, all left to head home. I'd taken Elaine into the hospice early morning, and we both spent time with Kevin. Then I left Elaine with Kevin, so they could spend some time together. I returned later to the hospice to collect Elaine and drop her off at the station to go home.

Kevin was well, so I felt I could leave him in the late afternoon to spend birthday time with our Janet. I knew he wouldn't have it any other way. I then went home, and Becci arrived from the hotel to stay with me for a few days before travelling to Leeds to see her daughter. Me and Becci went to the pub for Janet's birthday celebrations. Unfortunately, Liverpool only drew with Shrewsbury, so there's a rematch, which we later won, and then drew to play Chelsea.

Monday, 27 January 2020

Bad day. Kevin had trouble breathing all day and into the night. The doctor examined him and said Kevin had a pneumonia infection in his lung. He was put on a five-day antibiotic drip. I had taken Layla with me, I couldn't go home, I needed to be with Kevin. We stayed that night at the hospice, Layla on her rug, and me in the chair next to Kevin's bed. We couldn't leave him.

Tuesday, 28 January 2020

It was helpful that Becci was at home. I didn't see much of her as I was with Kevin, but she had the doggies for company, and they her.

Wednesday, 29 January 2020

Becci's last night, so we went for a meal to the '4 Tops', as Kevin called it (Four Topped Oak Pub).

Friday, 31 January 2020

Over the week, Kevin gradually improved. He was much more comfortable. What a week that was.

Saturday, 1 February 2020

Tommy and Josh came to visit Kevin. Kevin gave Josh the thumb's up as he left - wishing him well for his career in the police.

Sunday, 2 February 2020

Elaine and Dean visited.

Monday, 3 February 2020

I went into the hospice for 10 a.m. to be with Kevin when the doctors came in to see him. I think I need a separate talk with the doctors. I'm a bit confused, but perhaps everyone who deals with the symptoms, the next steps, of cancer, are.

The doctor tried to convince Kevin that sitting upright would be better posture for his breathing, but Kevin seems convinced it is not. I try not to push the doctor's advice as I know it upsets Kevin. And it's his life. But I really don't want him just lying in that bed. Whatever our life is right now, we have to make the best of it and live.

Tuesday, 4 February 2020

Phoned Kevin, and he was checking his emails to see if there is one from NS&I. I said I'd be in about 12.30. Kevin was a bit down when I went in. I walked into his room smiling to be positive, but it hurts to see him down. It was just a little thing; he had not had his wash yet at 12.30, but it was important to Kevin.

Our Janet was coming over about 2 p.m., so I went home to collect her and the doggies to go into the hospice. Returned them home about 4 p.m., and then I headed back, and stayed at the hospice until about midnight. Kevin and I listened to a match and watched *Whitehouse Farm*. I just need to spend time with Kevin.

They upped Kevin's morphine to help his breathing. It's heartbreaking to see him in discomfort. I sit in the chair next to Kevin's bed and softly play our music from Spotify on my phone while he dozes.

Wednesday, 5 February 2020

I finalised the letter to Ricky Gervais and sent it. I hoped he could pop in to visit Kevin. We think Ricky is so funny, honest, and true to what he believes in. Not sure he will have time, and certainly not sure if I've done the right thing by writing to him, but I wanted to for Kevin.

I'm still having pains in my head and back and feel exhausted. But I feel guilty even just thinking about that. Right. Our Janet is coming over again today, so off to hospice soon.

We had lovely day together. I know that sounds odd, but Kevin was well, and the following happened:-

I arrived about 1 p.m. and left at 10.15. During that time, Kevin was hoisted out of bed into lovely, big, comfy chair. We sat side by side and watched *Luther* on TV. Then the massage lady came in and massaged Kevin's head, neck, and upper back. He loved it, felt relaxed, and felt it eased his breathing. I was so happy for him. Then I washed his hair, again very relaxing. Then we continued watching *Luther*. Kevin was OK in his chair, so he stayed there while he ate soup for dinner. Back in bed, we watched *House of Games*, then *One Show*. At about 7.15, Kevin fell asleep. I sat quietly reading and watching Kevin while he slept. He awoke about 8.45, just in time for us to watch *White House Farm*

I drove home crying, realising things we will not do again; book a holiday, go to Millers for a lovely steak and expresso martini. ☹

Thursday, 6 February 2020

Colin and Margaret are due to arrive today. I went in about 10 a.m. to take Kevin some ironed PJ tops; I forgot them yesterday. I left about noonish to go see dogs and returned about two to wait until time to pick up Colin and Margaret from the station. I went to view a bungalow in Eccleston. It was not quite right. None of it feels right. I am just going through the motions of doing 'normal' things. I'm scared.

The visit was nice. I dropped them off at local hotel to the Hospice, (they wanted to be near) about 10 p.m. I will pick them up about 9 a.m. tomorrow.

I spoke with the doctor. She said Kevin is coping with the symptom-control meds well. The 'breathing' lady came to see him to show him some techniques for controlling his breathing. He had a panic attack last night and did not have the strength in his arms to pull himself up to sit upright in the bed. He felt he was choking and was very scared. OT came to see him and gave him a light elastic band to use to exercise his arms and perhaps get some strength back.

Friday, 7 February 2020

Picked Margaret and Colin up at 9.15. We went to Willowbrook, had breakfast, and spent time with Kevin. Kevin was short of breath this morning; he needed a drain and an aspirate. Margaret and Colin left at 10.45 to go back to London.

I went back to Kevin. The drain and aspirate were done, but he is really exhausted, does not look well, and his hands are purple. I'm scared. I sat holding his hand for a few hours while he slept. Then I went home to see the dogs. Then back to hospice.

Kevin is really not well. It's heartbreaking. His face squirms in discomfort, and he murmurs, 'Oh, God', though he says he is not in pain. When I say, 'I'm here', he gives me a thumbs up. And when I ask, 'What can I do to help you?' he replies, 'Help me die.'☹ It hurts that I am helpless to help him. I love him so much. ❤

I've bedded down in the lounge chair next to Kevin's bed. I was offered a bed in another room, but I need to be near Kevin. Kevin has settled a bit and is sleeping after an aspirate and a blue tablet under his tongue to help his breathing. I'm sitting next to him, listening to our wedding CD, watching his breathing.

Saturday, 8 February 2020

I got home from hospice about 8 a.m. Our Tommy had stayed but already left to go to work. All the family are there if I need them. I go out with the dogs to the field. Then I take a shower so I can get straight back to Kevin.

I got back at lunchtime. I took the Valentine card that I had ordered online in the week. It arrived today, so took it in. He loved it.

Then, Dr Rachel came about 12.30 to tell us Kevin may not have much longer. Again, you never believe it. Well, I didn't. We spent some time talking. Kevin did a 'last post', as he called it, on Facebook. Yes, the 7-2 poker hand–the worst off-suit opening hand in poker, calling for a fold—was all his doing. Funny, brilliant Kevin, even after hearing what we just heard from the doctor.

I phoned his sister, Elaine, who was due to come tomorrow. She said she would come over and arrived about 7 p.m. During the afternoon, they were easing Kevin's breathing with more morphine. He was never in any pain, just discomfort with his breathing. I sat, held his hand, and talked to him all afternoon. I stayed the night, and although they had kindly brought in a bed for me, I just sat on it and held his hand all night. Elaine was offered a bedroom on site, which was comforting for her to be close.

I didn't want Kevin to go. How could he? We are one, and I can't be without him.

Kevin Left Us Sunday, 9 February 2020

Elaine and I sat and held Kevin's hand all morning, talking and sitting on either side of his bed. At 11.15 he took a few sharp breaths, and his body could not, did not want to take anymore.

I love you so dearly, my Kevin, more than words can ever say. So go, be at rest, wherever that may be. But you will stay in my heart always, forever, and ever. XX

The Willowbrook Hospice staff are beyond nice. Their compassion and care and love for us, and all their patients, is impossible to put into words. We waited with Kevin until they came to take him from the hospice. Farewell for now, my love.

Life in Little Steps and Big Hurt: Diary Log Continued

Week Commencing 10 February 2020

Dying is complicated, but everyone—the funeral director, the registrar, and so on—are so nice. As Kevin said recently, they must go to 'nicey, nicey school'. Family stayed with me until Tuesday. Then I needed space at home with Bess and Layla.

We chose a blue coffin, Chelsea FC colour. I was really pleased with that for both Kevin and his dad, lifelong Chelsea fans. I'm taking Kevin home to Ottershaw for a final farewell from our life of twenty-eight years together.

Getting the death certificate was, well, too final. So final it hurt, I wasn't expecting the emotion I felt. Our Tommy took me there for that, not something anyone should have to do on their own.

Over the last few days, I managed to catch up, without crying, on the phone with all my special friends. Life for the past six weeks has been door-to-door hospital and hospice, and I wasn't going to miss a moment of being with Kevin. But now I have those moments, minutes, hours, days.

Friday, 14 February 2020

Facebook memories brought up a picture from five years ago—Kevin, my one and only Valentine. Happy Valentine's Day, sweetheart.♥ ♥ My valentine always and forever. I'm so glad the card I had for you arrived early, and you saw it.

I'm taking Bess and Layla to doggy day care this afternoon. It's a start. Just a few hours to see how they get on in readiness for when I take Kevin back home for his farewell. Our Janet is coming over to go with me. I'm fine, but I think she would like to go. Then she is staying over. Suppose I'll have to have a wine or two.

Sunday, 16 February 2020

One week ago, my lovely Kevin left me at 11.15.

I spent time with family today, and that was fine. But then it hit me. Alone in the evening, thinking, feeling sad, and alone, I thought I was doing 'OK'. I could have had fifty people with me, and I would have felt the same - sad and alone. Evenings are when Kevin and I sat and spent time together. I miss Kevin so, so much.

Monday, 17 February 2020

It's a new day. My heart does not ache so much today, but I have things to think about and do, starting with the doggy walk.

Then bad day. Had to go into Liverpool, and the bus was late. It was a long journey into Liverpool, I need to have my wedding ring fixed. Felt alone, upset, I just wanted to get home to the doggies. I felt sad.

Tuesday, 18 February 2020

I went to see Kevin. It didn't comfort me like I thought it would. It is not my Kevin, but it is, so I won't leave him on his own there.

Ordered flowers, Ace of hearts.

Gill came to visit. We had a nice natter with cuppa.

Wednesday, 19 February 2020

I have things and things to do, keep busy. Sharon and Sophie are coming over tonight.

Thursday, 20 February 2020

Doggy day care trial again. Susan and Tommy are coming to see Kevin at the funeral home. They brought over a tasty chicken pasta for our tea (dinner to you, Kevin).♥

OMG! The OSC (Ottershaw Social Club) did the most amazing tribute to Kevin tonight, a minute of silence to remember him. And this is what was said:

> The evening of poker started with a minute of silence and quiet reflection for our very good friend and OSC Poker League founder Kevin Hughes, who sadly passed away on 9 February. He leaves behind his wife, the lovely Diane "Shuffle up and deal" Hughes, who founded it with him. He will be sorely missed by many of us. Diane and Kevin moved up t'North a few years ago but still popped down from time to time.

> Kevin's wake will be at Ottershaw Social Club. It is a poker Thursday, and yes, the poker league evening will still go ahead as planned. It is actually quite fitting knowing how much Kevin loved his poker, and we're sure he would not want the poker evening cancelled. For one

night only, as the day is really all about Kevin, we plan to leave the position he usually sat in at the poker tables vacant as a further mark of respect, remembrance, and tribute.

♥

The following picture shows Kevin in June 2017. He had won both the OSC Poker League and the OSC Final.

Saturday, 22 February 2020

I had a nice time at Leanne's and Grace's joint fortieth and eighth birthday parties held at their lovely home with family and friends. At first they were not going to have it, and they asked me. Of course they should; life goes on. I managed not to cry! Our Janet came home with me and stayed over.

Sunday, 23 February 2020

Went to M&S to collect slippers. Kevin bought me a lovely pair of red slippers for Christmas, and they fell apart. When I took them back last week, the same slippers were £4.50 more, something about a different supplier. Hey M&S, get real. Customers only know what the item looks like, not who supplied it to you! Anyway, they gave me the new pair for the same price; Kevin wasn't letting them charge me more. They only had the blue left, so in the end, perfect cosy chelsea blue feet. Thank you, my love.

More farewell arrangements have been made. The music—I did cry with this, but it was a comfort to listen to our music. And I know he was there with us - me, Layla, and Bessy. I even made a chicken roasty dinner for one. It was a bit odd doing that for the first time.

Monday, 24 February 2020

Our Tommy went to see Kevin. I dropped the doggies off for their first overnight stay at the kennels. When it's time, though, only Bess will be staying at the kennel. Layla will stay with her regular dog sitter, our friend Hazel. Tommy and I went to Church View Inn for the '2-for-1' dinner. Came home to watch Liverpool v West Ham. We beat them; get back to London, Hammies. Couldn't go out to Basil's. Not ready for that yet.

Tuesday, 25 February 2020

Collected Bess and Layla. All went well. Took the train to Liverpool Town centre to collect my wedding ring. I need that back so much. The printers came with draft Order of Service and the enlarged picture of Kevin I will frame for the church service. I messed up the picture by trying to fit it into the lovely frame Margaret and Colin bought me last birthday. Will get another print of the picture.

I have a feeling of loneliness in the evenings. I tell myself to brush it off. Got to get used to it.

Wednesday, 26 February 2020

Awful wet weather. Doggies walked and now to sort photos of Kevin's life for the slideshow at the club farewell. Ray and Catherine will do a collage of the photos I send them into a music/photo tribute. They don't realise how much they are really helping me.

Thursday, 27 February 2020

Couldn't sleep last night. Saw 4 a.m. Got up and made hot milk and did some admin. The dogs are not 'appy. If I'm up, they are up! I am so stressed about the photo collages for Kevin. I should have ordered them earlier. Starting all over again with another online printer as the one I was going to use could not deliver until 6 March. The farewell is on the fifth!

I took Bess & Layla to the field this morning. Two big dogs came out of nowhere. They were OK but pinched Bess's ball. I couldn't get them away from us, and their owners were in the distance. I started crying. It was all just too much.

I went to the doctor about my bad hip. Got in there and started crying again.

Need to phone the funeral directors about Janet's visiting time tomorrow to see Kevin. I need to phone the other funeral directors down South about the cars. I can't let Kevin take his last car journey in a Volvo. I hope they can help, but it seems unlikely. So, so sorry, Kevin.

Yes, I am using two funeral directors, those looking after Kevin here, now, in Widnes, and then those whose care we will be in down South.

Took Bess to overnight stay at the kennel. I didn't want to but have to. Had to cry on way back to Tommy and Amanda's for tea. I kept telling myself to stop it, but couldn't. I got there and took deep breaths, stop crying. Tasty pasta and broccoli, and it was nice to see Josh there too. I left at 9 p.m. to go home; needed to go home. I cried all the way home. It's OK now home, back with Layla, but miss Bess.

Friday, 28 February 2020

Today feels like a better day. Collage's online printer, promised urgent order delivery. Walked dogs and Blackie. Had a friendly chat to Jackie on field with Oscar. She lost her husband six years ago.

Finalised the order of service. It was nice to talk to Marian, the printer. She is a lovely lady. She told me I was inspirational. Not sure about that. I just keeping going, wanting to ensure Kevin has the fitting tribute he deserves.

Our Janet came at 4 p.m., and we went to see Kevin. Susan and Tommy came over when we got home, and we all went to the Four Topped Oak pub. It was nice, but we just stayed for meal and then home.

Saturday, 29 February 2020

Kevin starts his long journey home today. It was on my mind every minute of the day. I kept busy, gardening, cutting back bushes, filling green garden bin. Then I finished putting the easel together. Kevin's picture sits nicely on it. It will stand at both the crematorium and the church services. Liverpool lost against Watford, and Chelsea drew against Bournemouth.

Sunday 1 March 2020

Popped in to see Sharon today. So, so glad our paths crossed, when both started working for the same company. In life, I believe our paths are already mapped out, I wonder, I believe. I came home and spent a few hours putting together some thoughts of our twenty-eight years together for Kevin's tribute page on *Much Loved*. I just felt I needed to share, but the words are a drop in the ocean in trying to describe our life together.

Had a bad night. I was watching TV and suddenly wondered, *Is Kevin in the office or gone for a lie down?* Then I realised neither. Sad.

Monday, 2 March 2020

It's four in the morning, I miss Kevin.

The florist phones and asks if I can collect the ace of hearts flowers between 11 and 11.30. Kevin died at 11.15, and here I was, collecting flowers around same time!

Tuesday, 3 March

So, the day has arrived. I'm starting the journey I don't want to start, but I have to. Friends down south tell me it's sunny. That's a sign; Kevin loved the sun. It's raining here. I'm on my way, sweetheart.

It really hurt leaving Bess at the kennels. Watch over her, too, Kevin.

Terrible weather going down south. The rain is pounding the motorway so much I'm unable to see the white lines. Then I got onto M25, and the sun shone through the clouds at J14, Heathrow, as if Kevin was saying, 'You're back with me, and you're safe.' Then at J13, 'Suspicious Minds', one of our favourite Elvis songs, came on the radio. Kevin was definitely letting me know he is with me.

Dropped Layla off with Hazel and had a chat. She's such a lovely lady. We're so lucky that she took on Layla's doggy minding over the past many years.

Left Hazel as it got dark and again raining. I arrived at the Premier Inn. I couldn't find the entrance (which I now know is at the rear of the building), got quite distraught, but then found it. It took four trips from car to room. Just like old times, eh, Kevin. (whenever we went away within the UK, we travelled with some apparatus needed for wheelchair assistance, plus usual bags, hence the numerous trips I would make from car to hotel room).

Tricky arrived and then Ray and Catherine and Lesley and Sue. Thank you all you guys, I needed that.

Wednesday, 4 March 2020

Didn't stop all day. I didn't sleep well, up about 6.30. So I went for an early brekky. It was good to gather my thoughts for the day.

Made up photo collages in the morning, and then I went to Tesco to get some goody bags for the family— orange, water, choc chip cookies—just like I used to get for me and Kevin during our many, many stays at Premier Inns. Oh, and I went to Weybridge to get the birthday balloon for Josh, (nephew) birthday on 6th march, as I said, life goes on.

I went to see the Reverend Sandra at lunchtime and dropped the order of service at Roz's house. It was really comforting to talk to Sandra. I feel she is my guiding light for tomorrow.

Then I went to Lesley's for a coffee before dashing back to Premier to await the first family arrivals, Tommy, Amanda, and Josh.

Our Tommy and I then went to see Kevin. Kevin looked 'well'. Sam, the funeral director, was so comforting, and he is a Chelsea supporter, so Kevin was in good hands. It really put my mind at rest as to all going to plan tomorrow, again there was someone there to guide us all.

I said my last goodbye to Kevin. 'Night, night, sweetheart. Let's do this together tomorrow. I'm with you all the way.'

'Night, dols,' I heard him say.

The family arrived; Janet and Alan; Susan and Tommy; Ian and Leanne; Tommy, Kate, and Ella; Elaine; Dean; Hayley; Gemma; Cooper; Grayson. I need you all, we all need each other.

Thursday, 5 March 2020: The Farewell

The day has arrived. I feel sick in my stomach, scared. I really don't want to do this. I miss you so much; it hurts so much.

Shaking, and my legs felt like jelly. I just had to keep my eyes on you, Kevin. I need to give you the best farewell. I have to, for you, for us, for the family, for our friends.

It's raining; it didn't stop all day. But that brought comfort to me because the day we married and become one, it rained all day—our wedding, our perfect day. I knew you were telling me the bookends of rain are for our lovely, happy, sunny twenty-eight years together.

For our friends standing outside the crematorium and saying, 'What awful weather', I felt a sense of, they were getting wet and did not realise they were part of our story of being together then, now, and forever.

Everyone, everyone said what a wonderful farewell. I'm so proud, so comforted. They all helped by being there, crying, laughing, and sharing.

Travelling far and wide to be there, thank you all.

Friday, 6 March 2020

It's a new day, a sunny day. Kevin's favourite type of day. He is shining down. I must keep going. But it is a scary day, my first real day without you.

We had a family birthday breakfast with our Josh. Can't beat a hearty brekky all together, and it helped me to know they were well fed before their long journey home.

I left the hotel and went to Ottershaw Park fields for a little me/memory time. Then I checked in at 'Hotel Gurney'.

Later I caught up with Richard, Fi, Julia, and Suze at The Castle, one of our old haunts. Many a bottle opened there!

Went round to see Roz in the evening, and she cooked a lovely meal. We ate, drank, and talked. We have shared a similar path, so I thank Roz for being there. Neither of us wanted to be on this path, and I know we will be forever friends.

Saturday, 7 March 2020

I had a cosy bacon brekky at Lesley and John's, (Hotel Gurney ☺). Spent midmorning to late afternoon popping to see friends Rich and Darran, Catherine and Ray, Rach and Ben, Becci and John. Then poker evening at Lesley's with Trick, Marcus, Sue, Lesley, and John. It was very nice, but I needed to go to bed as I was tired and felt alone, although I wasn't.

Sunday, 8 March 2020

I picked up Roz, and we went to church. It was a very comforting atmosphere. Then we had coffee and cake in the church hall.

Went to see Sue and Geoff, and left my case there ready for staying with them this evening.

Sue and I met Roz on the crossroads by Hunts haulage firm, and we went to the Ottershaw Social Club. Chelsea beat Everton 4–0.

I spent a lovely, comforting, familiar afternoon with Trick, Sue, Roz, Fi, Julia, Becci, and Suze—just like old times, but I knew it wasn't, because Kevin was not with us.

Monday, 9 March 2020

I went over to see Colin and Margaret. It was hard and so emotional., so much, too hurtful; I tried not to show it.

Met up with Gill and Dave, (their long time friends & neighbours), and we all went to The George Harvester restaurant. We then took the bus to their lovely social club. Again, it felt like living outside your body, going through the motions of 'normal life'.

Tuesday, 10 March 2020

Back to Liverpool, our other home today. I'm ready. Before I left, sat with Margaret, she has a lovely family photo album with lots of memories. Colin went off to Chelsea pensioners. I tried to reassure Margaret not to worry about her scan results. I will always be there for her and Colin. I told Kevin I would, and I will.

The first night back home – it hurts, it hurts, missing you, Kevin, missing you. I need a few days to, well, just need a few days or I will go under. And I can't do that for you, for the dogs, for the family, for the friends. I can't do that.

Wednesday, 11 March 2020

I had a dream last night, so real. You didn't die, you kept breathing; please don't stop breathing. There are no words to describe when that happened. In my dream, you recovered from cancer, you got better. Oddly, Dad joined you and was well again too; he did not stop breathing either. Then I woke from the dream in the early hours and saw your face Kevin, in the leafy pattern of our bedroom curtains. You are there. You are with me.

Went to see the consultant today about my hip. You did want me to, and I wouldn't while I was spending every moment with you. I couldn't miss a second of our time. Anyway, the X-ray showed an awful picture of a smashed hip, and I need a new one sooner rather than later. On the way home, I was driving towards a lovely rainbow – you. So I'm glad you know I've started the ball rolling to get that new hip. I need to walk our doggies forevermore.☺

Bad radio! I went out later with the dogs, and 'Miss You Like Crazy' was on the radio. Maybe a sign we both miss each other. So instead of feeling sad, I think it's you telling me we are together, always and forever.

Miss you soooo much. There is no medication for a broken heart. I switch off my emotions, a sort of barrier to block out the pain.

Thursday, 12 March 2020

I bought a foot rest from the charity shop yesterday, for Layla to use as a stepping-stone onto our bed. She is finding it hard to jump up so high. I washed it, got rid of the old stuffing, and restuffed with your clothes. You will be everywhere, even helping Layla get on the bed.

Spoke to Gill. I was saying how when I took the dogs out, I watch people going about their lives. I asked, 'What is it all for? And why?' She understood and feels that too sometimes.

Sitting at PC writing in this diary, suddenly I look into our bedroom and notice the headboard is wonky. I go in to straighten it. Most likely it is not a sign, but maybe it is. I straighten it, and stand and look at our bed, remembering the good times, before cancer; where you slept, where you laughed, where you had breakfast and spilt tea and crumbs over yourself, where we watched TV and put the world to rights.

I especially remember the fun memories of watching the 'old fuks', as you called them, on TV, Sky News for the press preview, we put the sleep timer on the TV most nights and happily drifted off to sleep, knowing we would both be there next day. That won't happen now. But I did watch the old fuks last night. Why does life carry on? Why are we not together? Why did you have to leave me too soon?

Friday, 13 March 2020

Another day. Had another dream that someone had found us a new home. All we had to do was go sit and have coffee and cake while they moved all our stuff from Widnes to the new home. Then we just had to move in. But the dream was only me and you sitting and having coffee and cake, not the new home.

Spoke to the DNs. I want to send them a thank you card for all their kind help over the past two years.

Got the funeral director invoices. All paid. Again, they were so, so kind and caring.

Issues I Had to Deal With

Just about to phone regarding premium bonds. Hope it goes smoothly. It didn't! Apparently due to the amount we have in Premium Bonds, they need probate to transfer, release the funds. Why didn't they say that in January, when Kevin spoke to them from his hospital bed. I am upset at their lack of compassion, information, and because Kevin tried to ensure things would run smoothly for me when dealing with this.

I spoke to the private pension provider regarding Kevin's pension. Upset again. I need proof of my identification and a certified copy of the will. Why do these institutions need so much?☹ It seems like they are blinkered and have no compassion.

I did the ironing. That hurt because I realised I wouldn't iron any of your clothes again. Then I opened a bottle of red and listened to your 'Farewell Kevin' music – 'I never knew love like this before', by Stephanie Mills. Thank you, Kevin, for the twenty-eight years of love.♥

Saturday, 14 March 2020

I can't find my driving licence! Not the end of the world. I went online and ordered a new one for £20. Spoke to all the family today. I'm trying to start sorting out Kevin's things today. Silly, but even throwing away his flannels hurts. It's like I'm losing more of him. Maybe I will leave the sorting for now and carry on tomorrow.☹

Then Fi and Julia rang. They are such lovely, funny friends. Thanks, girls. Right call, right time.

Sunday, 15 March 2020

I have completed the first garden mow of 2020! And the one and only daffodil appeared. Who could that be? It's sunny, perfect to sit out with a bit of summer music. But I can't without Kevin.

Feeling hurt, sad, alone. Thinking of the coronavirus in Europe. The scenes on TV of coffins is really scary and upsetting. What is happening? What will happen? Seems the hospitals are being overwhelmed. Scared.

Monday, 16 March 2020

Braved driving into Liverpool to show the pension provider company confirmation of who I am! Got back home super quick. The coronavirus is in the United Kingdom. So scared.

Friends are What's App, texting, talking. That takes my mind off it. I need them all more than they probably know.

Tuesday, 17 March 2020

Returned the disability car, Kia Niro, back to Chapelhouse, St Helens. Was very sad, not because of returning the car, but because I was losing more of Kevin. Very sad.

Wednesday, 18 March 2020

Bad day. I was thinking about the car yesterday, not because of it going back, but the memories of when we got the train to Birmingham for the motor show, spent two days looking around, and found the Kia Niro. Memories of when it arrived on our drive. I can still see in my mind Kevin sitting in the driving seat. Didn't help when I took the dogs to the field - that song 'I Never Knew Love Like This Before' was playing on the radio again.

Then I received the 2020/21 council tax bill, saying single-occupancy rebate. That upset me - 'single occupancy'. Then I decided to try again to sort out some of Kevin's stuff. I can now understand why some people keep rooms, even their homes, as a shrine to their lost loved one, possibly because it just hurts so much to move it out. Had a well-needed glass of wine and then got upset even more. But thank you, Amanda, for the lovely Aldi Organic Vino rosé spumante. I was keeping it to enjoy when I'm settled in our new home, to raise a glass for Kevin as he loved that wine too. But I felt the need to open it tonight. Listening to the farewell music - Solsbury Hill.

There was more on TV about the coronavirus. Feeling frightened. I wished Kevin was here to talk to. But then not as a shiver runs down my spine thinking about what would happen if he was going through chemo or in the hospice at this time.

It is difficult to stop crying when you are crying so much. You just can't stop, can't breathe. You can't phone anyone, they can't help.

Roz is right. It does get worse.

Bereavement

Don't tell me that you understand.
Don't tell me that you know.
Don't tell me that I will survive,
How I will surely grow.
Don't come at me with answers
That can only come from me.
Don't tell me how my grief will pass,
That I will soon be free.
Accept me in my ups and downs.
I need someone to share.
Just hold my hand, and let me cry
To show me that you care.

Part of a poem by Joanetta Hendel. So poignant. I can't ever move on. I can try to move forward but never move on. You cannot prepare for grief. You must live through it.

Thursday, 19 March 2020

Today was a better day. Another day has dawned. Took the dogs out, and walked Blackie. Nice to say hello to doggy walkers.

The probate solicitor came to the house. I sat across the table. Due to COVID-19, we kept apart, but I need to sort this out. It's sad because I know Kevin tried to ensure all the paperwork would be in order to save me any hassle. So I'm sad thinking about this. Don't worry, Kevin. You did more than your best to save me from doing this. But you know me. I will cope.

Bess has been looking at me with that look again. That, 'Where is my dad,' look, it is killing me. It hurts so much. I try not to cry, and then I cry because we all miss you. That's what I can't cope with.

Friday, 20 March 2020

I dreamt last night that you came home, and I'd already started sorting out your clothes, and some of your drawers were empty. I'm so sorry, so sorry. I want you back. You are never and will never ever be out of my life.

Saturday, 21 March 2020

Went to see Ian, Leanne, the kids, and Cookie. Just on doorstep, at a two-metre distance, it was still nice to see them. Then popped to see Susan and Tommy. We sat outside, again two metres apart, with a cuppa.

Got home and M&S flowers were delivered. Oh no, where was my head? I put our address instead of your mum's when I ordered them for Mother's Day. I was so upset. What can I do? I was going to drive down to London with them. Then I googled a local florist in their area. A lifesaver, phew. Then it dawned on me that you used to buy me cards from the doggies for Mother's Day. Was it you who got me flowers, knowing it would sort itself out, and your mum did get hers. Odd I ordered them for delivery today. If it had been tomorrow, it would have been too late to order more. I would have been so upset that I couldn't get more flowers quickly delivered to your mum. I think I would definitely have driven down to London!

More sorting, then some wine, then some of our music and tears streaming. It hurts so much.

Tommy and Amanda came round for an hour this evening. It was lovely to see them.

Sunday, 22 March 2020

It's Mother's Day. I phoned Margaret; she got the flowers.☺

I feel so alone, so alone. It feels like there is no one outside. I looked through the window when it got dark just to see lights on in houses around us. I am feeling really emotionally fragile. I need you more than ever. I need you, Kevin, to be here with me.

The news on TV today talked about halting some chemo for patients. I'm upset to hear that for all those who need it. And it could have been you! Not fair, so not fair. OMG, how would you, we have coped. I didn't want you to go, but what might have happened does not bear thinking about—consequences of COVID-19 during chemo, in the hospital, in the hospice. All unbearable to think about.☹

Monday, 23 March 2020

I woke up with that sad, sinking feeling again, like a lift dropping in my stomach. I reach out to hold Kevin's PJ top. It brought some comfort, and sadness and tears. It was the last piece of clothing he wore, so I call it Kevin. I think of the song, 'I Say a Little Prayer', and get up.

Then at 8.30 p.m., Prime Minister Boris Johnson announces on TV that the United Kingdom will go into lockdown at midnight.

Tuesday, 24 March 2020

I wake up and reach out and kiss and cuddle 'Kevin'. Get up, get on with the day.

I go to bed and start crying. Why are you not here? What is life without you? There is no purpose.

I turn the TV on -LG TV—life is good – appears on the screen. LG is the brand name for Lucky Goldstar, and their strapline is; life is good, but I hate seeing this each time I turn the TV on because life is not good.

What is this coronavirus? Are we all going to die a horrible death? I need to protect the dogs. I need to be here for them. Oh, Kevin, they need me. Who would look after them if I die? I'm scared, so scared.

Thursday, 26 March 2020

It's a dream. I want, I need to wake up now. Is Kevin really not here? I couldn't find 'Kevin' PJ, and panic. There it is, under my head! Kiss and hold tight.

Lesley put memories on Facebook of three years ago (2017), before Kevin and I left Ottershaw. We were at Woking Theatre for a show, *Crazy Joe's Music at Nashville*, with Lesley, Tricky, Geoff, and Sue. We both wore our check shirts. We liked to get in the swing of any event we went to. Thanks, Lesley, it perked me up. The following photo shows Kevin, me, Lesley, Geoff, Tricky, and Sue at Woking Theatre.

I feel upset. I'm waiting for 8 p.m. to go outside and clap for the NHS and other support/key workers. The NHS did so much for Kevin. I went outside and cried.

Friday, 27 March 2020

I wake up and kiss and cuddle 'Kevin'. I do that every morning now. Even Bess has a sniff of the PJ top. Interesting. It's not fair that we are alone. We don't like this. We need Kevin.

Our Tommy popped by on way home from work. We just sat in garden, six feet apart, for thirty minutes.

Then, then, poker saviour! I joined the online OSC home poker group. I called myself Ethel Walsh. Kevin used that name when he played online back in the early 2000s to make others think he was a little old lady, and hence, a pushover to beat. This was before the OSC group at the club. Wish you were here to play online too. You would have loved this. I miss you all the time. I just played one game as although I enjoyed it, I kept thinking of you, and got upset, so needed to stop playing.

Saturday, 28 March 2020

As usual, I drove the dogs to the local field today, but I was stopped by the police as I drove into the car park. They asked what I was doing out in the car. I explained I cannot walk to the field, too far, I have a bad hip, and two dogs, one that pulls on the lead. But they said I should not be out in the car except for urgent journeys. I'll take your death certificate and my hip op. letter with me tomorrow. They may be flexible. Poor Bess needs her run around the field, our garden is too small.

Sunday, 29 March 2020

I had that dream again, that I was sorting out your clothes. I dreamt that I got rid of your socks, and you came back. You came in through the front door, as if you had popped out of the house. I panicked. I was confused. I had to put them back. I couldn't let you think I was throwing them away.

Got pains in my head again today. Gotta get through the day.

I go to bed and have that sad emptiness in the pit of my stomach that makes me cry. It hurts, the love and loss I feel, hurts. Our love for each knew no blips, hiccups. Disagreements, yes, but we were always strong together.

Monday, 30 March 2020

I had a bad night. Last saw clock at 4 a.m. I just felt sick in my stomach, missing Kevin. Then another dream. Kevin was in the hospice, and he drew his last breath. Then a few minutes later, he was breathing again. He was back with me again.

Colin phoned to say they received the Ensure drinks that I had sent to them – they were left over from what Kevin did not use. I really hope they help his mum.

I empty the wash basket, Bess comes to me as soon as I pick it up. She used to like Kevin's pants dropping out so she could chew them. Poor thing, she still remembers. It breaks my heart.

Tuesday, 31 March 2020

All dogs walked, so I sat for quick cuppa in front of *This Morning*. They did a piece about everyone dancing in their living rooms and sending in clips of it. It was so lovely and warming. They were even dancing with dogs. Then I started crying as they all had someone. Most days I cry about something. Today it was dancing on the TV. I must get a grip.

Heard this on TV and thought how lovely:

> We must be willing to let go of the life we've planned so as to have the life that is waiting for us. (Joseph Campbell)

I think I can let go, but never can I forget.

Wednesday, 1 April 2020

Did not sleep well again last night. Kevin in my thoughts.

Colin and Margaret's fifty-ninth wedding anniversary is today. I spoke to Margaret. She is still in pain, poor thing. She talked about a DNR and asked if Kevin and I spoke of that when he was in the hospice.

I'm thinking about Kevin's birthday coming up, just sitting and putting some words of tribute together to honour him for his birthday. Our Tommy brought me some Cobra beer as I said I have a chicken korma meal for Friday. Kevin and I always went out for an Indian meal and had Cobra beer on our birthdays. It's looming. I'm scared, but I'm not.

Friday, 3 April 2020

It's Kevin's birthday—the first one without you.

At 2 a.m. I put Kevin's birthday tribute on Facebook. I went to bed, put TV on, and lo and behold, there is Worf, our favourite Klingon from *Star Trek* franchise, and the one Kevin met while waiting in the gift shop at the end of Star Trek ride in the Las Vegas Hilton. Myself, Susan and Tommy, had been on the ride, but it was not accessible for wheelchair users. If that is not a sign that Kevin is with me, what is?☺♥

Our Tommy and Amanda had also done a Facebook tribute, 'Starman', by David Bowie. Tears streamed down my face. Kevin is my Starman and always will be.

There was lovely texts from Becci and other friends, lovely sentiments, and many more on Facebook. Such lovely, caring family and friends. Tears streaming ☹. Ahh, lovely picture of Ian and Kevin. I can't put into words what Ian posting that picture meant to me. Thank you, thank you all. XX

Sunday, 5 April 2020

Lovely chat with Margaret. She is so brave. Margaret saw a white feather in her garden, so I know Kevin is with his mum and dad also.

Had a nice, distanced, visit from Tommy and Amanda. We sat in the back garden and chatted. These are challenging times, difficult ways of living we are not used to.

I did a bit more sorting out in Kevin's office. Wow, zillions of cheque book stubs, back to 1989! Envelopes galore, enough to start my own stationers! Kevin used to say his grandad was a hoarder with carbolic soap. Just different times. Love you, Kevin. Miss you so much.

Early-evening PJ time, just me and the girls. Watch a bit of TV and have a little cry. It just hits me, a painful sense of separation. I watched the Queen's address to the nation from Windsor Castle, ending on, 'We will meet again.' It made me cry again.

I received a surprise call from Pam G. We had a lovely, warm chat. It cheered me up.

Monday, 6 April 2020

Start of another week and more isolating. Scary, Prime Minister Boris Johnson was taken into intensive care at St Thomas Hospital (across the river from Parliament). Scary. C'mon, Boris, you can pull through.

More sorting. Was going through Kevin's PC emails, and so on. It felt good to read his words, comforting.

Zoomed with Pam S and our Janet. Made one of Kevin's favourites for dinner, corned beef hash. I bought two tins of corned beef from M&S back in December as I thought it would be a treat for Kevin that I made it with the best corned beef. He never got to taste it. Sad.☹

Just feeling emotionally fragile again today, like on the edge - crying all the time. I can't; it upsets Bess.

Tuesday, 7 April 2020

Watching a TV programme showing lovely walks in Cheshire. I can't. I can't do it without you. I can't imagine going anywhere or doing anything without you. I miss you like crazy. I feel so much, so much pain in my heart. I went to bed but couldn't sleep. I opened the fridge to get the milk to make some hot milk, and tears started streaming. It hurts so much. It was the bad hurt that gets out of control, and you just wanna do something to make it stop. My whole body is consumed with sadness.

Wednesday, 8 April 2020

Another day ahead. Reading the SIA (Spinal Injuries Association) magazine, and it seems unreal not to think about 'accessible' transport, accommodation etc, after all these years of that being the be all and end all of our holiday arrangements. I've cancelled the monthly subs. Perhaps I shouldn't have, but, Kevin, I think you would say yes to that. In the magazine, there is an article on volunteering. I want to help, but I can't at the moment. Again, I'm scared to go out. Crying so much I can't breathe.

Can't sleep again. Up until 3 a.m. Did ironing at 1.30 a.m. That upset me again, as I had no clothes of yours to iron. Pains in my head. I noticed Tricky's on What's App, so we had a chat. That helped.

Thursday, 9 April 2020

Up at 8 a.m. I need to go to Co-Op store at nine, before it gets busy. Got home and wipe the shopping with antiseptic wipes as I take it out of the bag and into the house! I'm scared it carries COVID-19. I'm also leaving the post on the floor for a day, not touching it! Scared it carries COVID-19.

Played online poker this evening with the OSC group. (that's covd friendly) They have no idea how much it means and helps me just to see their names around the table. I don't even care if I lose.

Friday, 10 April 2020

Spa day Zoom with Becci, Rach, and Catherine – I sat in the garden to do this - lovely sunny day.

Bess loves being in the garden. I was in and out. Then in the early evening, the best time, I sat outside. I started to get really sad again while listening to our wedding CD. 'How Wonderful Life Is Now You're in the World'. And now you are not, so it's not wonderful. What am I to do? Then Tommy, Susan, and Tommy called on WhatsApp video. Just what I needed.

Saturday, 11 April 2020

I'm going to do a BBQ today with fillet steak. I'm thinking I might get upset (Kevin always BBQs the steak). Had Zoom with Susan, Tommy, Tommy, Amanda, Ian, Leanne, and the kids today for almost two hours. It was really good to see them.

Did BBQ and got upset. It just hurts that Kevin is not doing the BBQ. He liked to organise the bricks and light it. Then I drank some wine, listened to our music, still in the garden where we loved to be. It hurts.

Wednesday, 15 April 2020

I've had bad few days and not much sleep. Had phone calls from family and friends, and yes, I said I was OK when asked how I am. And I am, mostly. Then I go to bed and think. I'm not OK. My mind races, and it hurts.

Sorted my wardrobe today and I am quite pleased—twelve handbags and a black bag full of clothes for charity. I deserved a wine. I ate the chicken from Monday and settled down to watch the movie *Yesterday*.

Thursday, 16 April 2020

Sorting Kevin's office, still. I find his project work going back to the nineties. It is both warming and upsetting to see his handwriting on it, and it reads like a maths formula! Kevin was so clever. He should be here to enjoy life after working so hard for so many years. It's not fair. Found his MENSA certificate.

I couldn't play poker. My mind is not in the right place, and I'm feeling sad.

Bed and TV, but I still saw the clock at 3 a.m. Got up, made hot milk, and took some Nytol. Gosh, not much left. Can't run out of that! So much going round in my head I can't rest or sleep. I keep wondering if I could have done more for Kevin or if I should have done this or that. Should I have pushed him to go on holiday, spend weekends away? We just concentrated on the cancer the last two years. It's a hurt that I can't explain because it hurts like nothing else.

I have pains in my head and wake up. For a nanosecond, life is normal. Then it's not. Kevin is not beside me.

Friday, 17 April 2020

I was watching *Criminal Minds* on TV. Kevin liked to watch that as well. There was a storyline. An FBI agent lost his girlfriend and she comes back from the dead, and tells him to move on with his life, to live life. Then the show plays the song 'Heroes' by David Bowie. Is that you, Kevin, a sign? Kevin's icon (well, one of them) - David Bowie. At age twelve, Kevin wrote his Christmas list for his mum and dad, and he asked for the *Stardust* LP (along with other things☺).

This is the Christmas list Kevin wrote, and also the LP cover photo. Had to share, I'm sure many family and friends can relate to writing the same sort of Christmas list at age twelve.

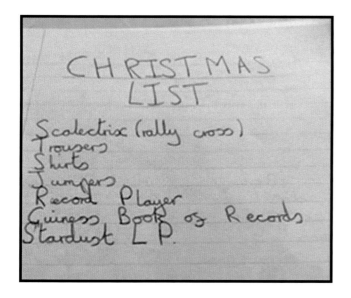 

One of our favourites on that LP was 'Starman'. Kevin, you are my Starman. ♥

Sunday, 19 April 2020

Had a bad few days. It's 'OK' during the day, but the evenings and night-time are quiet.

Susan's birthday is today. I have to shake out of it. I Zoomed the family. That helped.

Monday, 20 April 2020

I found Kevin's stamp collection today. I was really upset with myself for not finding it while he was in hospital as he spoke about it then. It was on one of the shelves in his cupboard, behind lots of PC gadgets, boxes, and so on. I so wished I had been able to take them to him. We would have laughed, and he would have reminisced. Very upset, I try not to cry because of the dogs.

Tuesday, 21 April 2020

I went over to our Tommy's, sat in the garden—social distanced of course. It was actually good to go out somewhere after four weeks of being at home.

Finished sorting the shelf of many wires in the office cupboard. Just need to know what is worth keeping. I don't know.

Ricky Gervais's cat, Ollie, died this morning, age sixteen. *Afterlife 2* is due on this week. I will watch it. I went to bed and had the most comforting dream, for a change. Normally there is so much going on in my head it pains me. In this dream, Kevin was beside me. My left hand brushed his soft chest; my right hand held his warm arm. It was so real. He said, 'You OK', as he always said. Then I woke. I didn't want to because as I gradually woke, I knew it wasn't real, and I wanted to go back to it. Then I realised the soft chest was the teddy bear on the bed, and his warm arm was his rolled up PJ top.

Wednesday, 22 April 2020

I'm sorting through the tall filing cabinet, looking at the 'accessible holiday' section. We saved so much information. Because we wanted to go to these places, we put in a lot of research into finding accessible holidays. We should have gone.

Thursday, 23 April 2020

Today is Tricky's birthday. Had a Zoom with them, Becci, Fiona, Julia, and Suze. It was lovely.

Pauline from Macmillan phoned me this afternoon. It was good talk with her. I told her how the days were not so bad, but the late evenings and night-time were not so good. She is a lovely lady.

Played poker at 7.30 p.m. Then I went outside, crying. I wish Kevin could be here to play too. I feel so, so lost without him. But I got myself together and decided to play 9.30 p.m. game to take my mind off just sitting and crying so much, I can't breathe. Watching Layla in garden having a difficult poo made me laugh.

Lockdown and grief together are hard. I haven't really seen anyone at all during this time, apart from the odd time in gardens, but never long enough to talk and get upset in front of them, which is good for them. At least on my own I can let it all out and I can sob and sob, and not bother anyone. They can't help, I know they want to, but they can't.

Friday, 24 April 2020

Watched *Afterlife* S2 and started crying. To make it worse, they played the Carpenters' 'Top of the World' song. Will continue to watch it as Kevin and I watched Series 1. I cheered up when they interviewed the one hundred-year-old woman, Kevin would have laughed so, so much. (a must watch, Season 2, Ep 1.)

Then Captain Tom was on TV, and they did a mix of lots of people thanking him. I started crying again. Don't know why. Or maybe I do because life is hard but beautiful as well.

Sunday, 26 April 2020

It's a sunny day, and I mowed both the front and back gardens. The weather forecast is not good for the rest of the week. I really wanted to be with friends, family—for drinks in the sunshine – just feel so alone. Treasure the one you are with, just the 'one' is enough.

Doing dogs' suppers. Put bowls on the floor. They really are my saviours. I go to fridge to get milk for my bedtime cuppa and start crying. It just hits you that life is not the same.

How I feel is difficult to put into words, but a low, sad, empty feeling in the pit of my stomach sends a wave of sad, tingly feelings around my body, through my legs and arms to my toes and fingers. My whole body is consumed with sadness.

Gemma sent picture of Grayson with a T-shirt on saying 'I'm going to be a big brother', and she said, 'Exciting times ahead.' I'm really pleased for them all, but I really don't feel like my life has exciting times ahead. I only see a blank sheet without Kevin. Each day is get up, get through the day, go to bed. Then I worry I won't sleep. And it starts all over again the next day.

Monday, 27 April 2020

Met family at the crematorium with flowers for Dad (almost 7yrs ago we lost dad). Though socially distanced, it was really good just to sit there with them and chat.

Came home and played poker with The Haven gang. It got me through the evening. It was good to be with them. Andy set up the other online poker group for our Haven Gang, the original crew. Thank you, Andy.

Tuesday, 28 April 2020

I found a lovely letter Kevin had written to his grandad, who he called Poppa. Kevin must have been about seven years old. It was so lovely to read. Here is the letter.

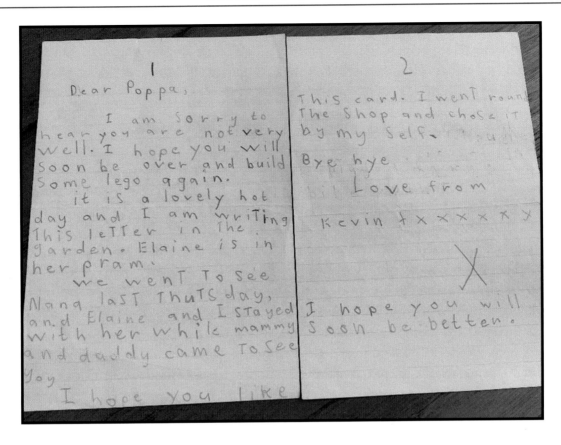

I've been sorting through the final drawer in Kevin's cabinet. It has his old work files. Gosh, he did so much—and kept so much. I am so proud of my Kevin.

I couldn't sleep. I sat up until 5 a.m. binge-watching *Gangs of London*.

Wednesday, 29 April 2020

I've been thinking of Dad. Seven years ago today we lost him. I got up at 9.30 a.m., so I had about four hours of sleep. But I needed to get up. Maybe I can sleep tonight.

Watched the final four episodes of *Afterlife* How can Ricky write something that so relates to me and I'm sure to many others who have lost loved ones. The grief feelings are surely all the same. Well I say that, but I know I felt a different sadness when Mum and Dad died than the one I'm feeling now after losing Kevin. In fact, Ricky mentioned that losing a parent is the natural order of things. Losing Kevin was not.

Friday, 1 May 2020

Is it May?

I had a few wines as it's Friday. When we lived in Ottershaw, I used to come home from work, get through the front door, and sing and dance, 'It's Friday; it's wine time!' Fun. Not so much now, just the wine.

It was an emotional evening. Maybe I shouldn't drink! I haven't cried in two days, but I also wasn't drinking. Then what the hell, as the *Afterlife* series says, drink when happy, drink when sad.

I've come to the conclusion the lockdown is definitely saving family and friends from seeing me uncontrollably sobbing. As I've mentioned before—often—sometimes I cry so much I can't breathe. And there is nothing anyone can help me with, so I might as well do it alone. No one wanted this virus, or lockdown, but it's given me a grieving /memory/healing time to go through alone.

There are different types of grief. I met my first husband at thirteen. We married at twenty-one, and he left me at twenty-six. That hurt, but it was a horrible, short hurt.

Lost Mum and Dad. That hurt, but it was a more steady, prolonged hurt, and I am forever saying, 'Wish they were here' to see this or do that.

Losing Kevin, well, it's been fewer than three months. It hurts, hurts so much I don't know what to do. That sounds odd, but that's what I say when I'm crying my eyes out from missing Kevin. I cry and cry, and say to myself, 'I don't know what to do. I don't know what to do without you.' I think of the future but can only see a blankness. I can't see anything. I don't want to do anything without Kevin. If I try to go on holiday, I just know by how I feel when I think about it now that it will hurt. So I don't want to go. I can't think about a new home (Kevin said I need to get out of renting; he hated paying for something that was wasted money), but I'm scared to take the next step. Where will I live? How will I make a life there without Kevin? I'm scared. It's not fair, it's not fair, why are you not here.

Can't stop crying. My leg is killing me. I drag it around, and it often gives way under me. Life sucks. The girls are sleeping, I couldn't leave them. How do people manage without dogs? Bad day.

Sunday, 3 May 2020

I went to see Tommy and Amanda today. Again, It was good to go somewhere for an hour. Days are OK, but I get home and the nights hurt. I feel sad and cry again! I try not to let Bess & Layla see. As Ricky G said, 'Keep it together; face the world.'

What am I to do? I sound like Cilla. But yes, she lost her husband, Bobby. I know her pain. I don't think she knew the 'hurt' meaning of those words when she sang that song, she still had her husband then.

Monday, 4 May 2020

I spoke to Susan. She is worried that her NRI levels are high. She has to go for an ECG. She sounds very tense on the phone. It upsets me that she is worried, but I can't deal with it. I know she is worried, and I'm sympathetic. It's just me, the way I feel.

I got off the phone, and it rang again. It was our Janet. I couldn't help myself. I was upset and just started crying. I feel emotionally fragile. I don't want to be, but I can't control it.

Tuesday, 5 May 2020

I spoke to Elaine. Not great news for Margaret (Kevin's mum). The chemo tablets have not worked, and her cancer has grown. But they are trying a new tablet starting next week. There is hope where there is life, and we must be positive

Played Haven Poker tonight with Sue, Andy, and Mike. I feel I'm really with them even though it is online. They really don't know how much it means to me to just be with them, playing poker and chatting. It's a comfort and helps me. But it also hurts because I think of Kevin, who would have loved playing with us, the old gang, again.

Wednesday, 6 May 2020

I went to the tip (recycling centre) at 8.50. There was already quite a queue at that time! But I'd taken *Eddie* to read, (an amazing book and brilliant gift from Fi and Julia). Two hours later, I got in, I had nothing else today, and at least I could see people!

I came home and took the dogs to the field. Lovely. Well define 'lovely' as a normal thing I need to do for them.

I phoned Margaret. I tried to be positive despite the bad news. We talked about Kevin's mementos, including the letter to Poppa. We had a laugh. I told her I would bring them down, and we could laugh and cry together. We love him. We miss him.

Spoke to Sue A at 7 p.m., then I spoke to Lesley, lovely chats, and then had what's app chat with Tricky. So good to catch up with friends. I want to be beamed back to Ottershaw!

Then I phoned our Susan to ask how her ECG went.

Then our Tommy phoned me and caught me crying. So he dropped in. Thank you, Tommy, but you or anyone do not need this. I'm grieving, but I know you are too, we all miss Kevin.

Friday, 8 May 2020 - It's VE Day.

I went to the crematorium to tidy Mum's and Dad's grave. Then I went to see Susan and Tommy. We sat in the garden for little while. All OK.

Amazing VE day celebration show on the TV in the evening. Such lovely, heartfelt, brave stories – very uplifting. A proud show in a magnificent setting and beautiful songs. Made me cry. At the end of the show, they said, 'Make the best of things, and keep smiling.' The best advice.

Saturday, 9 May 2020

Had a nice Zoom with Sue, Becci, Rach, Ben, Jenny, John, Pam G, Fi, and Julia.

Then I sat in garden for a late-evening wine and cried. I miss Kevin. It's not fair, not right. Why is life like this - so cruel?

Sunday, 10 May 2020

Lovely to see family on Zoom. COVID-19 restrictions relaxed, but it's still out there and still scary.

Monday, 11 May 2020

I went for a COVID-19 test.

Tuesday, 12 May 2020

Received my COVID-19 test results—negative.

Wednesday, 13 May 2020

Again the word 'OK'. What does it really mean? We ask each other, 'Are you OK'. We answer, 'Yes, we are.'

Every night I go to bed and say out loud to Bess and Layla, 'Another day done.' Every morning I wake up, and for a nanosecond, Kevin is there. And then he is not.

I think a lot. I look at our photos a lot. I remember our life together, our times at The Haven—normal days, party days, fun days. I remember our holidays, our celebrations. I remember time spent with family and friends, time spent at the OSC, time spent playing poker. Why, Why, Why did this happen.

I cry a lot. Sometimes I laugh at *Gogglebox* and then remember you are not watching it with me. I can't even watch *Turning Point* as I know it will upset me because that was 'our' show, we always watched it together.

I miss you, Kevin. It hurts, this unbearable sadness I don't know what to do with. or how to cope. I switch off my emotions, put a barrier between my head and my heart. Then I take a deep breath and plod along in life. I don't know how else to cope.

Thursday, 14 May 2020

I am sitting in the garden. I need to. The dogs love being out. Bess comes over to stand by my chair for a back rub. She loves that. I look at the ramp—memories. I see Kevin wheeling down it.

I cry, I cry. It hurts; it's not fair. Then more thinking:- Kevin's last Christmas, Kevin being given two to five years to live in May 2018. It's not fair. Why did he only get the two years. He would, and we would, have done another three years on chemo and more. And who knows what new medication, treatment, and so on would have then been available. Not fair.

Friday, 15 May 2020

I ventured to Tesco today. I felt brave and needed to potter. I was very COVID-19 organised. It felt good to be out. I made homemade spag Bol, one of Kevin's favourite dishes. I sat down with it on my knee, looked over at Kevin's picture, and cried.

Saturday, 16 May 2020

I had nice hour sitting in our Susan's garden—and a glass of Prosecco.

I'm in a better mind space today. Our Tommy phoned on his way home from work. That really helped me.

Sunday, 17 May 2020

I had a bike ride and then made three shepherd's pies out of a tray of mince. Kevin and I would have had all the mince in just one pie. Things are very different.

Wednesday, 20 May 2020

Took the Doblo in for service. Took the bike in the back of the car and cycled home.

Netflix is still playing up. I spent thirty minutes Tuesday onto Netflix, and thirty minutes today onto BT. I miss my 'techy guy' and had to cry. It just gets to me. I cancelled Netflix!

Went to sit in the garden and enjoyed watching the sun go down. I tell myself to stop it, not to start crying again. But I can't help it. I miss Kevin. He would be watching the sun setting with me.

Thursday, 21 May 2020

I cycled to pick up the car today. It needed new brakes and shoe things, but it is all serviced and safe. Tricky joined the Haven Poker team tonight. It was a really good game. It gave me a lovely feeling to see them all around the table.

Sat in garden after. There was a lovely warm breeze in Widnes, even at 11.30 p.m. I phoned Tricky and had a nice chat. Then I sat some more and had a little cry. It's been an up-and-down day. I miss Kevin. XX

Friday, 22 May 2020

Janet is coming over today. We had a nice BBQ and a few glasses of wine. All good.

Saturday, 23 May 2020

Elaine and Dean came today. It was really good to see them. We went through some of Kevin's things that Elaine was happy to take.

Played poker with the OSC gang in the evening. It was a comforting game. Then I had a little cry.

Sunday, 24 May 2020

I went to Susan and Tommy's and had a lovely roast chicken dinner—distanced around the table of course. Spent two hours with them and then drove home. Had a little cry on the way home. It is lonely. I miss Kevin.

Monday, 25 May 2020

Felt sad, sad for another bank holiday without Kevin. I felt alone but have our lovely girlies. Don't get me wrong. I could have gone to family gardens for social distancing, but it's not the same. That's what I mean when I say 'alone'. I could be surrounded but still feel alone.

I listened to our music and text Trick and Sue. Don't want to sob and do the, 'Whoa is me.' It's not fair on them or anyone. It's my grief. Miss Kevin. XX

Tuesday, 26 May 2020

It's a new day, and I felt better. Went to B&Q 9 a.m. to get skin colour paint for Batesy. Batesy is the CFC gnome. Kevin named the gnome 'Batesy' after Ken Bates, who bought the Chelsea Football Club for a £1 in 1982. Our Batesy had fell over in the wind and broke, so I'm putting him back together and painting him. I have to finish him off to take to Colin and Margaret. I look at him, and memories flood back. But I know he will bring them comfort at this time. He stood on the patio at The Haven for many years, so I look at him and remember. Following are photos of Batesy broken and after being glued back together.

I bought a sunflower plant as well. I love them.

Thinking of Margaret today and the results of her scan.

Plodding on, I played poker with the Haven gang. Loved that, but then I feel sad and miss Kevin. It hurts like I can't explain. I sit on the sofa, watching TV, and my mind wanders, looking at pictures of Kevin all around me, wishing he was here. It hurts. Many times I have to rewind programmes because I can't concentrate.

Wednesday, 27 May 2020

Woke up crying this morning. I surprised myself with that as I wouldn't have thought it possible. There's a wave of sadness and feeling so low inside.

A smile can hide a thousand different feelings.

I couldn't sleep last night. First time in a while. Then I realised I hadn't taken Nytol. I was also worried because I hadn't heard from Margaret about her cancer scan results. Like last time, I thought perhaps she was too upset to talk, and I was too scared to phone her. I know Elaine would have spoken to her. But as it happened, a text came through on my phone the next day, about 10.30 a.m., but it was sent at 6.30 p.m, to say, 'No results today—delayed.'

What is the meaning of 'grief' – Google meaning:- intense sorrow or trouble/annoyance.

I feel both meanings are one. I have intense sorrow, and I don't want to trouble/annoy anyone with it.

I have to get through another day, so I get up and feed the dogs. But I just want to crawl back into bed. But I can't. Intense eyes are staring at me, saying, 'We want our walk.' Is that one solution to grief - get a dog?

We are like facade; we can have deceptive outward appearances. What you see on the outside does not determine what you are feeling on the inside. But then again, apart from non-grief and some other issues, some people feel normal, even happy on the inside, but their faces don't show it!

Falling asleep on the sofa, I say to girlies, 'Bedtime.' They go off out for a wee in the garden, and then their suppers. I go for wee and start crying, uncontrollably crying. I re-live that last Saturday, 8 February over and over again. (but really? crying on the loo, the sad feelings just hit me wherever I am)

You were not dying; you were never dying. I cry and cry. Dr Rachel was at your beside and I was on the other side. Her drawn face saying something about more pain relief. You knew. You said, '7-2 offsuit hand', but to me, you weren't dying. You were not. You were not. It felt like it wasn't happening, that it was something that wasn't real. So it wasn't to me. You were not dying, you were not.

Looking back now, I wished I'd said more at that time. But what I would have said would have meant you were dying, and you were not. You were not, so I couldn't.

I couldn't accept it.

Thursday, 28 May 2020

Another bad night, looking at the clock at 2 a.m. I took some Nytol and hot milk and didn't wake up until 9.30 a.m.

I decided not to rush, not to worry. I had no real agenda today. I would take time out.

I had nice Zoom with our Janet. I don't say all this obviously. I don't want them to feel upset for me.

Lovely pictures of little Andersons in the sunny garden. Joined in What's App chat posts -nice.

Playing poker tonight. Tomorrow another day. I hope to sleep tonight as I swapped Nytol for wine!

Won poker game heads up against Tricky and had a moment of joy. Then I sit on sofa. I need to leave Northern Lane as I get upset with ambulances driving past with sirens. It's near the hospital, so it's the route into it, but it reminds me of 2 January, when Kevin left Northern Lane in an ambulance and never came home.

Went into the garden. I hate to waste warm nights as Kevin and I were always in the garden. But he's not here, and I cry and cry cos he's not here with me.

Friday, 29 May 2020

Went to see a couple of bungalows in Formby. Kevin, if I ever needed your help, I do now, please. Going forward feels like I'm looking at a blank page, a mist I can't see through or past.

Saturday, 30 May 2020

Another day, another day. Had a really lovely conversation with Sue A this morning. Out of the blue we normally ask, 'Are you free?' I know I don't ask enough, and it was nice. She's worried. This COVID-19 is a horrible time for all. It was really nice to speak to her.

Spent few hours on the internet, bungalow hunting in Formby. Then our Tommy put the quiz on the family What's App. I enjoyed that; it was good fun. Good banter with all. Then I put Ian and Leanne's wedding CD on as today is their eleventh wedding anniversary. It was a lovely wedding. I remember Chelsea were playing, and Kevin was wondering what the score was. Such such happy, good times, and I want them back.

I listened to the CD—Sterophonics, Dakota—and then that low, sad feeling. Tears streaming, wanting Kevin back. It's not fair. Then the Beatles' 'All You Need Is Love'. I had love but not long enough. Not fair. Miss you, Kevin. XX

Sunday, 31 May 2020

Going to Tommy and Amanda's today for a nice roast chikky dinner. Did well. Didn't cry.

Monday, 1 June 2020

An odd day, the first of June. Just odd. What's it all about?

Tuesday, 2 June 2020

I had a bad, bad day. Just felt so sad, down all day. Didn't help that I had problems trying to retrieve photos from Kevin's moby via the Samsung Share viewer. It didn't work, so I need to take to Tesco for help. I can't lose them. Then the last few days my email kept telling me my mailbox was full. All a reason to cry and cry.

Wednesday, 3 June 2020

Better today. I spoke to a helpful man, Charlie, at BT. Basically, I need to start up another email account as Mozilla Thunderbird is on its way out! But he assured me I could keep the icon to check on information I had in folders on that site, a bit like an old filing cabinet. I knew this day was coming. It would be a nightmare to inform all those who email me, not just family and friends, but companies. Then I thought, Calm down. I can do it. As I receive an email, I can change email address back to recipient.

Thursday, 4 June 2020

Today was my first day back at work, and it was OK. I received a lovely welcome back from the girls, including flowers and chocs. All went as normal, When I got home, I played poker. That was good. Then I had a bit more drink. And then the sadness and crying hit me. I miss Kevin. It seems I try to take a step forward and then take two steps back. I miss you. Miss you. It's hard.

Friday, 5 June 2020

Our Janet and I went to see a few bungalows in Formby today. I know I have to, and I do it like a robot, a bit like each day, get up, whatever, go to bed. It's not the words 'moving on'. No definitely not. It's taking a step forward. Otherwise, I would stand still, hibernate. And I know I can't do that for the dogs.

I think I might draw the diary to a close as I now feel I'm just living a numb life and what I'm saying is repetitive. Like Sky News, it's on a loop, isn't it, that's what Kevin used to say.

Our Janet stayed overnight. Can't remember much because I was on sherry, but I think I must have bored her with, 'Whoa is me.' I don't mean to do that. Hence lockdown is good as I only talk to myself.

Tuesday, 9 June 2020

I went to see the bungalow in Watchyard Lane again today. I saw it October 2019, but it only had two bedrooms, so no 'office' room for Kevin. The interior was a bit tight for his wheelchair, so it was a no go back then. I feel guilty thinking it's OK for me now. I feel sad and sort of excited. It was not supposed to be like this, not at all. It will always be 'our' home. There will never be anyone who compares to you, although you did tell me to find someone. No, never in a lifetime, my lovely, funny Kevin.♥ We'll meet again in heaven, and my broken heart will be no more when we do. I know you don't believe in heaven, so you need to let me know where you are. We had something so special, a one-off. I'm trying to move forward, but I feel I'll never move on. Tears streaming again.

Thursday, 11 June 2020

Went to work and had a good day. But I'm not sure it's really the right job for me now. There are too many memories of:- you being diagnosed; going through chemo; being in and out of hospital; and then in hospice. All ran parallel with working there. Driving home, I just started crying. I miss you.

Played poker with OSC gang. Then I played with the Haven gang.

Got knocked out and I then sat down and started crying. Not because I was out, just the usual highs and lows of missing Kevin. I feel numb. It's like my head is outside my body, watching day by day as I wake up, do the 'day thing', and then go to bed. And it all starts again the next day. In between I cry so much I can't breathe. I miss you, Kevin. I don't know what to do except the numb thing.

Friday, 12 June 2020

I phoned Margaret, spoke to Colin. Margaret went to St Georges hospital last night. She has had back pain for a few days. When she spoke to her Macmillan contact, she was advised to go to hospital. Colin took Margaret but had to leave her at the hospital entrance. He could not go in. I feel sad in that instance for them both. Damn COVID-19.

Watched a funny What's App video of Rae and Grayson playing. It made me smile.

Gemma got engaged. Good news, very good news.

Had nice visit from Susan and Tommy in garden. It means a lot. Life is different.

After they left, I sat in garden early evening and felt sad, alone. Kevin should be sitting with me. I sit, look at the ramp and, and visualise him wheeling down it again, I almost see him; I do see him. Maybe I should stay in garden because that's what we both liked to do. I miss him, it hurts . I cried and cried and cried into my PJ top to smother the sound, I don't want the girlies to see. I looked out, and they were both looking at me! Bess with a tennis ball in her mouth, made me smile. Kevin sent them.

Saturday, 13 June 2020

I spoke to Colin. Margaret is home, but she is in bed. Poor thing, she has had mixed messages about her cancer.

Monday, 15 June 2020

I took Susan and Janet to view the bungalow in Watchyard Lane, Formby. They liked it. I just felt I needed more reassurance about it because I'm on my own. Then we returned to Northern Lane and had a nice few hours, the three of us in the garden, cuppa & cake.

Tuesday, 16 June 2020

Things are rolling along with the solicitor. I spoke to Margaret. She seems better, sort of. She will see her consultant at the Marsden Hospital on Tuesday.

Wednesday, 17 June 2020

I was boxing up Kevin's clothes that I want to keep, along with the cufflinks I got him when we got married, and a pair for our anniversary. Also a holiday bum bag, and white Vegas cap, which he wore continuously on all holidays.☺♥ But, I couldn't find his yellow polo shirt. I see him in that, in my head, all the time. Where is it? I wouldn't have thrown it away. I also couldn't find the Christmas card he got me last Christmas, our last Christmas together. (As I read this back, I found the card in the Christmas tree box in December. Phew!) But things I can't find so upset me.

I played poker with Sue and Tricky tonight. It was fun, just like being with them.

Then another bad night. I felt sad, felt like I couldn't go on. One part of my head says I must, and the other part asks how?

I was awoken at 3 a.m. by a clicking sound. I jumped up out of bed, but there was nothing clicking when I got up. Maybe it was a dream. I let dogs out in garden, made hot milk, and went back to bed. I dozed off and woke again at 5 a.m. Totally awake, I got up. I feel sad and down, highs and lows, the roller coaster of grief.

Thursday, 18 June 2020

I received the solicitor pack! Going through it, I miss having Kevin to help. There is so much paperwork. I can do it—I have to—but I feel alone reading and completing it without you, Kevin. I'm having pains in my head. I really feel I will be joining you soon. It just feels that way. I can't see a way forward without you.

Sunday, 21 June 2020

It's Father's Day. I sent a card to Colin. I think today will be very, very hard for him.

Popped in to see Sharon on way home from work. I may have a new car (well 2017 registration) by the end of next week. Sean, Sharon's son, has been helping me find a car. I feel guilty and upset at buying a car. But at the same time, it means I can travel back down South again.

Our Tommy and Josh picked me up to go watch the match, and we had a lovely roast chicken dinner and Eton mess for afters. Thanks, Amanda. It was lovely to see Josh. He starts his police training in August.

Tuesday, 23 June 2020

I had a nightmare last night. Or was it? I was in bed asleep, and in my dream, it felt like someone was hugging me from behind. I was too scared to turn around. My sister Janet was staying the night in the next room, so I tried calling out for help. But I couldn't shout loud enough, it was like a muffled shout. I couldn't muster any noise, which was scary. But, was it Kevin hugging, reassuring me? Please come back if it was you. I'm sorry; I just got scared. But on thinking about it today, maybe it was you.

Played Haven poker this evening and then a tele call with Trick. I miss him. We talked about his mum loving the song 'Time to Say Goodbye' by Sarah Brightman. There were a few tears from both of us.

Woke up in the night. After hearing on the radio today about African chiefs who, hundreds of years ago, sometimes sold their own people. I dreamt I was in an African village. People were running around with machetes. I was sitting on the floor crying. 'No, please. No, don't!'

What is going on in my head!

Thursday, 25 June 2020

Liverpool became Premier League Champions after thirty years. It was a great night for all the fans who had waited so long and those who were not born the last time Liverpool became champions. There were quiet celebrations at Northern Lane. It was very quiet. Even Layla was snoring, but the TV coverage was fantastic.

It was a mixture of sad and happy for me. Chelsea sealed it for us—thank you, Kevin. I remember lots of footy times gone by at OSC with our footy-mad friends. And the pound bets between Mike (Man U) and Kevin and Andy (both Chelsea) being pushed around the table.

Friday, 26 June 2020

Chasing the estate agent to see if the seller has passed along his solicitor details after nearly two weeks! It's a bit stressful. I believe in, 'What will be, will be', but this bungalow looks just the job and the right place for us, Kevin.

Saturday, 27 June 2020

Benidorm, Spain - that didn't happen. It was booked pre-Covid, and obviously cancelled. Around at Sharon's instead for a much needed afternoon/evening like we had with fun, laughter, drinks, and friends. That's what's important in life.

Monday, 29 June 2020

It was a busy day. Halton Council collected Kevin's two spare wheelchairs and accessories. I'm keeping the one he was using; I can't part with that, not yet. Then the PC man came and took Kevin's four tall PC boxes, four screens, and six keyboards. Again, I've kept one.

Then Sharon and Sean brought over my new car, a 2017 Nissan Juke. It's lovely. I can't get excited, though. It's a car to get me on the road to collect you from Ottershaw, and bring you home. We went into lockdown a few weeks after the funeral, so I had not been able to get back there to collect Kevin's ashes.

Tuesday, 30 June 2020

Drove to the field looking at your picture on my sun visor, the song 'Fame' playing: 'I'm gonna live forever'. Tears streaming. Why couldn't you, Kevin.

More Issues to Deal With

I received a letter from the pension provider (A). They need a certified copy of your will, our marriage certificate, and your death certificate. I need to send it all to them by recorded delivery. It's the certified will that has upset me. How much paperwork do these people need at a time when it is really upsetting? Upset again, feel so tense, and crying. These companies need to reform as to what is required. What is the point of a certified will? The fact the original Will is signed by two witnesses should be adequate!

I just seem to be making phone calls, filling out forms, contacting people, and so on and so on. Feel emotionally exhausted.

Wednesday, 1 July 2020

Another day, another month. Went to work today. Driving home, I passed the chippy (chip shop – Chinese Lucky House) I used to stop at and get us fish and chips. I'd ring you to turn the oven on, and put the plates in.

I looked at your picture on my sun visor, and tears streamed.

Thursday, 2 July 2020

Had a nice visit from Janet Also, Liverpool lost to Man. City - not so nice! Our Tommy popped in.

Sunday, 5 July 2020

Played poker online with the OSC gang. I do enjoy it, but then I cry my eyes out. I miss Kevin. It's hard to carry on, to live without you. It hurts so much.

Tuesday, 7 July 2020

Went to the Willowbrook charity shop in Prescot today to take Kevin's clothes. It's not like taking your old clothes. Taking them, in this instance is … well, those who have done this will know what I mean. It makes me feel like I'm taking a step forward and ten steps back.

Our Tommy helped me. We had three large, heavy bags and a suitcase full. It was a suitcase we used on our cruises. I only need one suitcase now … if ever. So, Willowbrook is best to have these as they looked after Kevin so well.

I had a sad feeling with Kevin's clothes. I've kept what meant something to me. But, Kevin was so funny. He would wear the same polos, shirts. I even tried putting his favourites on the bottom of the pile on the shelf. He would pull them out off the bottom to wear, so I kept those. But over the last month, I kept going back into the black bag and suitcase to take more clothes out to keep! It feels like I'm losing a bit more of Kevin by giving his clothes away.

I went to Susan's this afternoon. I planned to pick her up, spend a few hours here at Northern Lane, and Tommy would collect her. But bad weather and with COVID-19, she won't come into our house. So I went up there as I'd baked scones for us with clotted cream and jam. I couldn't eat them all!

Home with girlies. I cleaned and bubble-wrapped pictures around the house, getting ready to move. I got an email from friends, Jean and Thelma. They reminded me that Kevin had seen this bungalow from the property brochure, as I had viewed it in October 2019. So, he knows of it and where we will live. It made me feel better to remember this.

But then, I showered and just started crying and crying and crying in the shower. I miss him. It hurts.

I went to sit in the garden. It was wet weather, but not cold, I was under the umbrella. Birds were singing, and it felt fresh. I cried again. I'm writing how I feel in my diary. I don't want to pester family and friends; they can't help. It hurts.

Then Layla and Bess had a scrap. I think Bess senses my hurt and misses Kevin as well. Poor Bess; poor Layla. I stopped it as soon as it began.

There is no rule book on bereavement, no guide. I'm not the first and not the last by any means. It is individual. And you can, and will cry, even if you think you are strong. Whether you have been in love a day, a week, or many years.

I went to write in my diary tonight, and I thought I'd hit on 'diary' to open the document. But Kevin's picture opened instead. He is with me. He knows I need to write about how it feels, how I feel.

The previous picture was taken in Brighton. We went there often because we loved the sea, the coast. We always took the dogs, from Skip to Sky to Layla, and Bess. We would buy the fresh donuts on the pier. There were five in a bag, two each for me and Kevin, and one for the dog. We loved to walk along the promenade and then sit at the Peroni Bar on the beach.

Wednesday, 8 July 2020

Worked a shift today. Didn't really want to go. I've sort of lost enthusiasm. Zoom with Pam S tonight. Looking forward to 'seeing' her.

It was a restless night. I woke up early, and my face just crumpled and I cried. I hugged you (Kevin PJ top). What am I going to do? Where am I going without you? What am I to do? I pulled the duvet over my head so I don't upset Layla and Bess. I just feel like staying under the duvet forever and ever.

Friday, 10 July 2020

Again - Friday reminds me that I used to come through the front door after work shouting with glee, 'It's Friday.' The dogs would come running, and Kevin said, 'Cheers.' I'd open the wine, and the weekend would begin. It's not the same now. But I sat out like we used to in the garden on a Friday, in the summer, before we went to the OSC, Bess sat right in front of me, as if Kevin was telling me he was with us. So many tears, so many tears.

Kevin happily playing with Bess and Layla with a Friday night Bacardi and Coke (Diet, of course). This was taken in August 2017.

Saturday, 11 July 2020

I got a new phone today, Tesco mobile. Just like Kevin's, a Samsung.

Tommy came over in the early evening. I did us a couple of steaks on the barbie, just like Kevin and I used to have – the memories comfort me. I was gonna do one for myself anyway, before he had said he was coming over.

Then Tommy drove me to the Welly, (Duke of Wellington pub) by where they live, where Amanda and her friend were. I was bit dubious about going out, both with COVID-19 out there and because I was scared I'd start crying and spoil the evening. But I enjoyed it. It was the first time I went 'out, out' in about nine months.

They dropped me home, and then I felt very sad. I cried listening to David Bowie. I miss Kevin so much.

Monday, 13 July 2020

I got a haircut, my first since about this time last year! It felt good to have a tidy trim, all accomplished in a COVID-19-friendly manner.

Tuesday, 14 July 2020

Saw Mr James F, hip replacement consultant, today regarding my hip. X-rayed again, and it still looks smashed. And it still hurts. Normally they would have given me a date for the hip operation, but due to COVID-19 and the backlog of operations, it would be six to eight weeks. I'm fine with that. It means I can go down South, in early August, collect Kevin, and see his mum and dad and our friends. I so need to do all that.

Becci joined the Haven poker gang. It was lovely all playing together tonight.

Wednesday, 15 July 2020

Watched a TV programme, *911*, last night. It dealt with someone dying. At the end, they said, 'We can spend our days trying to understand the pain, and we should, that's how we heal, but, we must always remember it's not the trauma that defines us, it's how we choose to react to it, how we choose to move on.' Wise words.

Thursday, 16 July 2020

My head is a bit out of it today. I did a few chores, ran errands, and made phone calls. But I forgot to go and walk Blackie! I realised at lunchtime and went and walked him then. Oh dear, get a grip, girl! I spoke to some friends, it was lovely to speak with them. I mowed the garden. Gotta be done, bad hip or not.

Friday, 17 July 2020

Today was Auntie May's funeral (Dad's sister). Went with our Tommy, Susan and Tommy. Our Tommy came back to NL for a quick drink. And then I was on my own again. Well not really as I have Bess and Layla.

Saturday, 18 July 2020

Just me and the girlies for the weekend. Gotta get used to it.

Monday, 20 July 2020

It's been a long weekend. Different life. I'm feeling numb again. Had nice online poker game with the Haven gang. But then sad. Highs and lows again.

I've been doing lots of thinking. Kevin was so clever. He was very humble. I feel his disability sometimes held him back. It was so difficult for him to go out to a workplace that was maybe not accessible, and to travel for work (nightmare train travel stories, I can tell you). Kevin worked all his life, both as an employee after leaving university, and then self-employed as an IT programmer.

More thinking; of the hospital times, the chemo times, the hospice, all these images, thoughts, memories hurt so much I have to stop thinking because I can't bear it. I can't cope with the feelings. It tears me apart. Words can't explain. I try to think of good times, fun times with you, and then I feel guilty because you are not here.

Tears streaming, miss you, Kevin, so much it hurts.

I want to fill our new garden with memories, like Skip's bench; Sky's rose; the water feature your mum and dad bought for our wedding gift; Dad's plant; Mum's plant; the hosta Bob gave us; Haven daisies. Then I can sit in the garden, see them, and think of you, the family, friends, dogs, and our life.

Friday, 31 July 2020

I spent the last week or so being really careful. I can't catch COVID-19! I need to go down to Ottershaw to see Margaret and Colin and collect Kevin. I need him home with me now.

Saturday, 1 August 2020

I drove down to Morden, Surrey, Kevin's mum and dad's home, non-stop. I was scared to use the toilets at motorway services!

It was a very emotional time with Margaret and Colin. Shame Chelsea lost at football. Showed them memory items of Kevin, which I had taken down. I gave Margaret the pink Kevin monkey. (I had bought these on-line from Love, Keep, Create – you send an item of clothing to make them out of).

Got some Slade Road Haven daisy cuttings from them.

I had a blue Kevin monkey. Both monkeys were made out of Hawaiian shirts he loved to wear. I added the Chelsea emblem to mine.

Photo of Margaret and 'Kevin' pink monkey

Photo of both monkeys

Photo of Kevin in both shirts

Photo of myself and Colin with Blue Kevin monkey and Batesy

Sunday and Monday, 2–3 August 2020

Spent time with Roz, Sandra (the vicar), Lesley, John, Mollie, Richard, Bob, Sue, Geoff, and Mike. It was really lovely to see them all in person again.

Roz gave me a beautiful bracelet with mine and Kevin's names inscribed on it. It was so thoughtful, and I love it. Sue gave me lovely flowers as she was thinking of us for tomorrow.

I collected Kevin. Colin came over for some of Kevin's ashes.

Tuesday, 4 August 2020

Today is our eighteenth wedding anniversary, but we had twenty-eight years together.

On the road home with Kevin's ashes, I cried a few times, and a few times more.

Margaret emailed me a photo of them laying Kevin's ashes to rest in their rose garden. It was emotional for them and for me.

Kevin's beloved Batesy watching over him.

Kevin's home, and I am relieved.♥

Janet was at home waiting for me and stayed. Tommy popped in. Received comforting cards, with lovely sentiments. All the family have been so supportive.

Wednesday, 5 August 2020

The solicitor phoned me. There's a hiccup on searches with regard to the extension, something about the building certificate. This is so stressful, but if I'm not meant to have the bungalow in Formby, then Kevin will guide me, and I will accept that. My hip really hurts too. I know there are awful things going on in the world, especially the Beirut explosion, but it doesn't stop you from feeling stressed and upset with your own bubble of challenges, which also seems much bigger when you feel emotional and stressed.

I gave Elaine some dates last week to try and pop over to see them, but I have not heard yet. They had a nice gathering in a pub garden for Grayson's first birthday. It looked lovely. I hope to see them all soon.

Saturday, 8 August 2020

I went to Leeds to visit Elaine and the family. It was a lovely afternoon in the garden. Made me smile, as I can hear Kevin saying, 'Jesus Christ. Noisy kids!', it was good to sit among them and listen to the chatter, the kids playing, but I felt alone.

I was a bit upset when I got home. Again, the highs and the lows. Thinking, thinking, thinking of that Saturday six months ago, when Dr Rachel seemed to say it was nearing the end. Even then, to me Kevin was never dying, never. I don't know how people say goodbye when they get that news.

Sunday, 9 August 2020

Went to work and came home. Sharon and Sophie came round about 4 p.m. for some drinks in the garden. Having friends around really felt good, like old times. But after they left, I cried my eyes out because Kevin wasn't there, like he used to be when friends left. These are all new steps, and they all hurt.

Monday, 10 August 2020

I am stressed about the new property. There is no news on the issue with the building certificate for the extension done in 2005. I feel like saying, 'Don't worry. I'll sign on dotted line to buy the bungalow', as it is so stressful, but I can hear Kevin saying don't, he would not do that. I have to be strong. Guide me, Kevin.

Wednesday, 12 August 2020

I met Janet and Jane today at the Punchbowl Pub. It is my first restaurant outing in months and months and months. It was a nice time. All COV'D organised.

Thursday, 13 August 2020

Got in the car to take the dogs to the field today, listening to the radio, I just started crying.

I went to Susan's for lunch alfresco. A few hours out, just what I needed.

I feel like the grief of missing Kevin is getting worse. I miss him, and it takes all my strength to keep my head above the sadness and despair of life, I'm struggling. I think I'm coping with grief, and then I'm not. It feels like I'm drowning in it! But I have to keep going.

In the Tramps song, 'Hold Back the Night', the words are, I suppose, more about a relationship break up than a loss, but just those words, 'hold back the night, turn off the light … I dream about you baby.'

I so need to get away to see Trish, so I'm going on Sunday. I've had a bad week, crying at the slightest thing, keeping my face on for lunch and other things. But I need to get away for a few days—two girls, two dogs, and lots of wine.

Thursday, 20 August 2020

It was good to see Trish and have a few laughs, a few tears, and a few wines. She is a good friend forever.

On the long drive down to Plymouth last Sunday, I was thinking - I do a lot of thinking.

Thinking about that word 'OK'. As said before, it is used so easily. And when asked, I feel like saying, 'No, I'm not,' but that's not nice. People mean well.

Thinking again about Christmas; I know I can't cope with being with lots of family. I know I will feel like I did at Elaine's the other weekend—sad, hurt, alone—like being there but not being there, just looking on.

Thinking about feeling tired; the last two years since we found out that Kevin had cancer has been a determined, driving force of positive adrenalin. And then the six weeks from Kevin going into hospital on 2 January, and then the hospice on the twenty-third, same positive adrenalin. So the five months since the farewell have been like an adrenalin 'come down'. Maybe, because as much as I try to rest, I just feel exhausted. I'm thinking It will get better in time?

While I was away, poor Bess had an accident in the living room. I don't think I'll leave her for some time now. I think she worries as I took Layla with me, and with Kevin not coming back, who knows what she is thinking, poor thing.

Good news from Margaret. The tumour markers are still low and responding to chemo, so no hospital appointment for two months.

Took Layla for a groom. She is now nice and clean, and smells beautiful. Went to get my nails done for the first time in six months.

Registered for poker tonight with the OSC gang. At work tomorrow and Saturday. Then the week starts all over again on Sunday. Going to Four Tops Pub with our Tommy tomorrow night. I'm looking forward to that - to going out, out.

Friday 21 August 2020

Had a lovely catch up with our Tommy, treated to a steak meal.☺ Had a chat about Christmas, just trying to help them understand how I feel. I can't be in one of their homes without Kevin this Christmas. It hurts, it will hurt. I just need to be at home with Bess and Layla at Christmas. Then I can feel Kevin with us.

A wadge of papers arrived in the post today, the thickness of an old yellow telephone book! It was new home contracts and other paperwork. It was scary and daunting. Kevin and I would work through anything like this together. I can do it, but I wish he was helping me. Completed it all and then Tommy & Amanda did a check over with me. I want to get it all back to the solicitor, so I can get a move-in date. I want to leave NL now. I feel numb. The good memories, and we definitely had some here, will come with me. Kevin will come with me to Formby.

Monday, 24 August 2020

Went to work. When I got home, I mowed the garden before storm Francis arrives. All day thoughts of tomorrow loomed over me. For the first time in twenty-eight years, I will wake up on my birthday without Kevin. I'm trying not to cry. Don't cry. I'll be fine. I've got Bess and Layla, and family and friends are visiting.

There are many signs that indicate those we love and lost are still with us:

>   White feather: The angels are with you and surrounding you right now.

>   Brown/black feather: Your angels are sending you love and support.

>   Butterfly: Someone in heaven you are missing is free of his or her pain.

>   Robin: A loved one in heaven wants to remind you of your strength.

>   Rainbow: A promise your loved ones will never leave you.

Tuesday, 25 August 2020

At 9.10 a.m., I turn fifty-eight years old. It is my first birthday without you, my first as a widow.

Bess and Layla jumped up on the bed to wish me a happy birthday. Unfortunately, they did not bring the cake and champagne we always have in bed on our birthdays. But the cake would not have made it to the bedroom! I put the card out that Kevin gave me last year. Why not? I will for years to come, and Christmas and our anniversary and Kevin's birthday. He is not here in person, but he is always in my heart, my mind, my overall being, and will be in our new home.

Long day on my own with the dogs, but I knew family and friends were coming later. It's all just different. I can cope. We all can cope.

The first to arrive are Janet and Alan. Then came Ian and Leanne, Grace, Jack, Tommy and Amanda, Susan and Tommy, Sharon and Sophie.

It was a lovely evening. The kids were gorgeously funny, happy. Just what I need.

Have packed most stuff away, so I had no candles for my birthday cake. We used long matches to put on top of the cake. Jack thought we were doing a fire show!

Thursday, 27 August 2020

Had a much needed natter and drink with Gill - my oldest friend of almost forty years. We met when we both worked at T J Hughes, Liverpool. Then, Gill went to London around 1985, and I went to London in 1989, and we always stayed in touch. So our friendship is Liverpool to London and back to Liverpool, for me.

Also received a phone call to say my hip operation will be on 16 September. I'm scared and glad at same time. It's gotta be done.

Tuesday. 1 September 2020

It's pre-op. They asked if someone is at home as I need someone there for a week after the operation. That question hits me hard. No, not anymore. But, of course, there is always family. I didn't expect that question, and it must affect many people like me. I cannot drive for six weeks. I wasn't expecting that either. I thought I'd go in, get a new hip, and be up and about within days, and back to life - whatever that is at the moment. I also have to stab myself with blood thinners every day for a month after the operation. That brought back memories of helping Kevin with that. I'll do it on my own.

I am counting on you, Kevin, to get me through this if that's what's meant to be. Or maybe I'm meant to join you. I've typed up what is to happen with Layla and Bess in case of the latter. I've also done a draft of my funeral arrangements to help those left to arrange it simply, and with ease. I'm scared as this is my first big operation.

I'm isolating for two weeks now prior to my operation. I am also trying to finalise packing up NL before my new hip restrains me—that's if I live to move to Formby. It still doesn't seem real without you, Kevin. I'm putting some boxes, and some other stuff that has been in the Northern Lane garage since we moved here in June 2017, into Tommy and Amanda's garage. There is no garage at the Formby bungalow, so I'm panicking about getting everything in the spare room. I will buy a PVC shed, but I have to transfer the garage stuff from one to another for a few months. Looking at the label on the boxes—Eternal Beau dinner set, Gold dinner set, dinner party serving dishes, and so on—are all things we used in our life at The Haven. We intended to use them again in our new life up North. When I was packing those boxes in May 2017, never in a million years did I think you would not see those items again. I cried, cried, cried.

Thursday, 3 September 2020

Kevin always remembered this date, it was the anniversary of his motorbike accident, so I will. Kevin was twenty-three in 1985.

Playing poker this evening, looking at your picture. Listening to sunshine by Gabrielle. I miss you, love you.

Saturday, 5 September 2020

Tears streaming. I miss Kevin. I feel guilty. It's not fair; he shouldn't have died. I don't know what to do without him. I miss him, and I feel guilty living without him. He didn't deserve to die so young. 'Starman' is on now. Is that you, Kevin? You loved that song. Are you trying to help me not feel so sad?

Sunday, 6 September 2020

Watching *Celebrity Gogglebox*. They showed the 1966 World Cup - Bez's friend Shaun asked, 'Who wins this game?' Very funny. I look at your picture cushion and think you would so love this. Laughing turns to crying. I want you to be here with us.

I played poker with the Haven gang. It helped me cheer up a bit, but I drank so much, I got really upset. Surprised myself at how much I drank. I have to stop it, but the grief just feels like it's getting worse. I cried so much my face was like an ocean.

I text Margaret. I shouldn't have; it was late. But I feel she knows how I feel, a mother's loss, a wife's loss, is different, but Kevin is our loss. I told her I missed Kevin so much and that I cry a lot. I told her that she had the best son ever, and I had the bestest husband, best friend forever.

Margaret replied that she cried an ocean when she read my text. I did not mean to upset her, really didn't. Margaret went onto say, 'Kevin was such a wonderful son and never complained of his illness. He will be in our hearts forever. And the tears will continue, happy tears, sad tears. He gave us so much joy.'

The loss of a husband or wife, I never knew, or could know, how that felt until it happened to me. Thinking back now of the friends we have who have suffered this loss, I'm sorry I wasn't there for you more.

Monday, 7 September 2020

A new day. I still feel so low. I've got to tell myself not to feel low and to get on with stuff. It's really hard. I just feel on the edge of crying all the time.

It's little Ella's first birthday, lovely pictures, beautiful little poppet, will see them soon.

Tuesday, 8 September 2020

I couldn't sleep again last night. I got up at 1.30 a.m. and gave the wok a good deep clean. I put the wooden bathroom cabinet back on the wall. We had taken it down when we moved into to NL because it was too high for Kevin to see in the mirror, and he would hit his head on it as he was lower, sitting in his wheelchair! so it was taken down and put in the garage.

Had a garden visit from Susan and Tommy. They brought homemade cheese pies. Yummy.

The solicitor confirmed the completion date for the bungalow is 25 September. Hope to exchange at the end of this week. That's some relief. I hope to sleep tonight.

Found my driver's licence. I thought I'd lost it while packing the filing cabinet stuff. It was in the divider file next to the file it should have been in!

Thursday, 10 September 2020

Had a lovely family Zoom. So nice to see everyone together. Then played OSC online poker. I won the first game and was second in the second game. That felt good. I felt Kevin would be proud of Ethel Walsh. Then looking at Kevin's photo made me cry. I cry lots all the time. It hurts so much being without you.

Watched *Criminal Minds* (S10 E15), on TV. Kevin would watch that show with me. The show ended on them having a leaving party and playing David Bowie's 'Heroes'!

The episode was very poignant:

> "There is an infinite amount of kindness in the world no matter how bleak it seems. The love you take is equal to the love you make. It's the end, of it all, it's the end of it all. All my friends at the end of the world I hope to see you again. It's the end of this time, it's the end of our time. Oh how little do we know, we had such a long way to go, when you sleep tonight you will be in my dreams. Soft dark kinda love, nothing comforting me, the earth went quiet, the air went still, I feel you know more than I ever will. Frozen in grief, the world needs you to do what you love. Your heart and guts know what is best, let them rule over your head. To be nobody but yourself".

Friday, 11 September 2020

Exchange day! There was a nightmare with transferring money from my bank. Long story short, the maximum you can transfer on a daily basis is £25k -bit short of the cost of the bungalow! I still can't believe we will get our forever home at last.

Monday, 14 September 2020

Roz came to visit. It was lovely to see her. We are both at different stages in our grief, dealing with losing our lovely husbands in our own way. Many thoughts, emotions, and actions are generic in grief, but our loved ones are as individual as grains of sand on a seashore, leaving those left behind to make sense and cope with the why.

Tuesday, 15 September 2020

Hip operation eve. I'm scared, anxious, and worried about Layla and Bess.

Wednesday, 16 September 2020

It's hip operation day. Our Tommy drove me to the Spire hospital. Gotta do this, tick it off the list, eh Kevin - you told me to. Settled into room, obs. done, anaesthetist chat, physio visit to sort out crutch size, lots of activity. Consultant came to see me; I'm second on the list for the afternoon. So I sat in my room and read my book, watching the clock. I should be going down about 3 p.m. But 3 p.m. came and went; 3.30 came and went. I was really feeling nervous. I was feeling sad, looking at the picture of myself and Kevin on the Azura cruise. It was taken informally on the deck in the cool evening air. Those were fun, carefree times – times I would never dream in a million years then, that I would be sitting in a hospital room, on my own, and you would not be here. At last, at 3.45, I was walked to the operating theatre area. Three anaesthetist staff were helping me, but it all got too much while they were giving me the needle in my back. I burst out crying. I was so upset, missing Kevin and feeling scared and alone.

Parties on deck   24 April 2011

Woke up at 6 p.m. in the recovery area. I felt OK. I was back in my room at 7 p.m. They gave me a tuna sandwich, but three bites, and I was sick. I felt really ill. I couldn't move my right leg. I was really scared, upset, alone. The staff helped me, but it just felt lonely.

Thursday, 17 September 2020

The physio came. It was so difficult to get off the bed. When I stood up, I felt horribly nauseated, hot, and clammy. I sat in the relaxer chair next to the bed for a few hours. Then I felt so tired and got back into bed. I slept for few hours in the afternoon, and when I awoke, I felt better. OK, so not so bad, but it was still such an effort to move my leg. And it was still difficult to get on and off the bed. I had to push my right leg with my left leg to move it!

Friday, 18 September 2020

I woke up and felt ill again. I thought I was through the worst yesterday! Was determined, though, and I had two physio sessions. I'm gonna do this. I need to go home; I have to go home. I felt upset again. In no way had it occurred to me that having this operation would be so traumatic, upsetting, and emotional. That all hit me like a ton of bricks.

Saturday, 19 September 2020

Ian is coming to collect me. I need to go home. I had a physio session this morning, and it felt better. But I need to go home. I had to wait for some meds—not long, about twenty minutes—but I was getting upset. I need to go home. When I finally got into Ian's car, I burst out crying.

Family on stopover rota for the week. Susan is staying tonight.

Sunday, 20 September 2020

It's Mum's birthday. Happy birthday, Mum. Sorry I can't make it to the crematorium today to lay flowers, but they will get there. (we lost mum in 1988)

Monday, 21 September 2020

For the first time since my operation, I could lift myself off the toilet. Doing that simple thing felt like I'd won the lottery! Got to get this leg working again.

Wednesday, 23 September 2020

I feel much, much better. Went for physio, and they are pleased with my progress. I'm now on just one crutch in the house to help me get around, instead of two.

Thursday, 24 September 2020

It's Completion Day Eve. I need to be on my own, need to think, remember—to be with you, Kevin, in my heart.

Friday, 25 September 2020

It's Completion Day at 150 Watchyard Lane. I have to go and get the keys! Had to be driven there as I still cannot drive. I'm having mixed emotions. Janet asked if I was excited. I'm not. It's a lovely new home, but Kevin, you were supposed to be there with me and Bess and Layla.

Susan brought cakes, so we had a cake celebration. I was so pleased the family were there to help me through this milestone.

Saturday, 26 September 2020

Going back to Formby, our new home, again today. Is it really our new home? I arranged with Removals to move in completely on Monday, 12 October, so I will spend the next few weeks getting it cleaned and taking bits and bobs up to Formby, with the help of the family as I am still on crutches, well one now.

Monday, 28 September 2020

Thinking about the move. It just doesn't seem real, not real, just going through the motions. I miss you, Kevin.

Wednesday, 30 September 2020

I'm at Northern Lane, sorting out BT service and thinking of Kevin as I sit in his office. If I could just have one day back with you … Just one please.

Thursday, 1 October 2020

Boxes to Formby. The house is taking shape, which is good. But I came home and cried. It's hard, really hard.

Saturday, 3 October 2020

I spent the afternoon with Ian at WL (Watchyard Lane). It was a lovely, relaxed time pottering in the 'new' Haven, chatting and getting some stuff done. Ian built a wardrobe.

Saturday evening, I'm sitting here back at Northern Lane with a glass of wine, thinking about it all. We came up North. What the fuck happened? Sad, sad.

Saturday, 10 October 2020

Just two more sleeps in Northern Lane. I can't believe it; actually moving. We spent the last years of your life here. We did have some good times, we did.

We left Slade Road, Ottershaw, together to start a new life. I'm leaving Northern Lane with Layla and Bess – and you in my heart.

It hurts. It hurts.

Monday, 12 October 2020

We've moved to Formby. We eventually get to live near the coast like we talked about doing five years ago.♥ It's a sad, numb day. The family are great, really great. They're all gone, so it's time to cry.

Saturday, 17 October 2020

It hurts. I miss Kevin.

Kevin should be here with us in our new home. It hurts. It's not real. Has he really gone? No, no, need you here.

Thursday, 22 October 2020

I think it helps in dealing with grief to be a resilient character. Fear, sadness - all emotions - try to harness them to get through. Try to focus on being positive before grief takes hold and has a negative impact. Life is humility and compassion itself.

Ironing. Crying again because I'm not ironing your clothes anymore. So many 'not real' things happen.

Saturday, 24 October 2020

Don't know where my life is going. I feel so empty and lost without Kevin. So lost it hurts. My head tells my body to get up each day, do day-to-day stuff, and go to bed. And it starts over again the next day. It feels numb.

Sunday, 1 November 2020

Playing OSC Haven poker. It's odd looking around me sitting here in our new home. Kevin, you should be here.

Friday, 6 November 2020

Finally handed back the keys to the Northern Lane bungalow. So sad you didn't move on from there with me and the girls. I'm glad to be leaving the area because of the memories of driving to and from the hospitals and hospice, and the sounds of ambulance sirens passing our front window.

Sunday, 8 November 2020

I watched my first Christmas movie of the season. I love Christmas and want to buy and decorate our usual real tree. But I know it will also make me sad as I'm feeling sad now just thinking about it. And it's still six weeks off.

Friday, 13 November 2020

I'm back to work. When I got home, it felt good to have been to work and have a schedule to my week again. Hot bubbly bath, glass of wine, and music, Whitney - when the night falls, the loneliness calls – so true.

Saturday, 14 November 2020

OMG! Our Janet has broken her shoulder! She slipped and fell in her own living room.

Sunday, 15 November 2020

I went to the beach again. It's lovely, peaceful, and blissful. Tommy and Amanda came. I think they loved it too.

Joined Ottershaw church 4.30 light service via Zoom. It was comforting but sad. It made me cry; I miss Kevin. But it was a comfort to be part of the church service.

But then felt so low, it was a bad evening. I cried a lot. What happened to our life? Do I keep asking this? I think I do, but I keep wondering why. And now what is life about? How do I go on?

Monday, 23 November 2020

I got that horrible feeling again, the sad emptiness in the pit of my stomach that really hurts, and there is no medication that will take the pain away. Christmas is looming. It is going to hurt not to have Kevin here with us.

Tuesday, 24 November 2020

I had nice little shop in the village with Susan. I'm mostly OK during the day. As usual, it's the evenings and night-time.

Oh no. Poor little Grace has been taken to hospital to have her appendix out.

Saturday, 28 November 2020

I went to visit Janet. I feel really sorry about the pain she is in. They cannot plaster the arm because the break is on the shoulder.

Came home and had some leftover curry from the takeaway the other week, which I had put in the freezer. I'm getting really good at not wasting food. It was delicious.

Then I watched TV, then went to bed. I had that feeling again. My whole body was consumed with sadness.

Sunday, 29 November 2020

Kevin's beloved Chelsea v Spurs today. Tommy and Amanda are coming to join me to watch it. Ended in a draw, 0–0.

1 December 2020

Christmas cards, I can't write them this year because they will not be from Kevin, Diane, Layla, and Bess. I just can't.

Wednesday, 2 December 2020

It is odd. I haven't seen anyone for three days except one or two people on the field of a morning. GMB TV today had a piece about 'lonely', and 'alone'. I think I've mentioned this before, but there is a huge difference. I don't feel lonely as such, just alone. But their piece highlighted that there are many people like me, alone for one reason or another, even with dogs. But I do talk to Kevin, constantly, so I'm OK. I also know I have amazing family and friends, I can call at any time.

Played Haven poker last night. That makes me feel I am with friends, and I am, over the internet. But I don't think they realise how much that means to me.

Sunday, 6 December 2020

Went back to Northern Lane today to pop an extra set of keys through the letterbox. I had found them while further unpacking. That was OK, but the drive on to work, ie passing the Observatory Pub - brought back memories of our walk home from there (pre-cancer), after playing poker into the early hours, and our sunny afternoons in the beer garden. Then passing the Hillcrest Hotel, where we sat outside in the sunshine with a bottle of red wine. Then passing Pesto Restaurant, where we had a lovely meal, finally passing the Church View Inn, where we had a lovely roast. All these memories made me feel sad and hurt. It made me realise that although Kevin is with me in spirit, he has not lived in this home in Formby. If he had, I feel the memories that would have been made, would cause more pain than that I'm already feeling, if that makes sense.

Then our Tommy and Josh paid a visit to watch Liverpool v Wolves. It was lovely to see Josh, he was home from Aberystwyth, Wales, for a short visit.

Tuesday, 8 December 2020

The Royal Variety Performance was on TV this evening. It's something that Kevin and I never really watched, but I did tonight. Well, I put it on thinking I'd switch to Netflix, but I had to keep watching. It was fabulous. Comical presenting by Jason Manford, amazing singing and dancing, emotional tributes, entertaining acts. It was very uplifting yet sad at the same time. 'Cilla' (Sheridan Smith) sang 'End of My World'. It feels that way for me. Then Michael Ball sang, 'YNWA' with Sir Tom for the nation because we need each other in these terrible pandemic times, and then 'Lean on Me' so we know we can, and should, on each other.

I'd watched Ray Mears on TV just before this, and that made me cry because I remembered when Kevin and I went to see him at Woking Theatre because we enjoyed watching his TV shows. However, we had had a few drinks before the show, and with the theatre being so big and dark, Ray seemed so small on a large stage, and we both sort of dozed off! So we sneaked out before the end as we couldn't keep our eyes open! A funny and sad memory.

Sunday, 13 December 2020

I went to work yesterday, and when I got home, a leaflet from St Peter's Church, Formby was on my doormat. Luckily Layla had not shredded it!

Bereavement service at 4 p.m. today. I went, and I cried. The sermon really related to my life with losing Kevin, so I'm not alone. (Well, I didn't literally lose him; he would laugh and say he is too big.)

I know Kevin would say, 'Don't be sad. Don't be sad.' Easy to say, but I'm gonna try not to be. St Peter's Church sermon mentioned that grief has a list of firsts—first birthday, first anniversary, first Christmas. So true. We get through the firsts like climbing a mountain. Then the seconds, thirds, fourths and so on, all become a bit easier.

I'm glad I went to St Peter's Church. It was a dark, cold evening, but the walk through the churchyard to the entrance was filled with Christmas trees lit up with bright lights. It was enough to make anyone going to a bereavement service smile. And I did. But when I got home, it hit me again – tears streaming.

Kevin would laugh at my churchgoings, as I also did Ottershaw Church Zoom at 10.30 a.m. today. 'Jesus Christ', he'd likely say, and he may be right. It's my way of—What's the word I'm looking for? Guess it depends on who you are—coping, comfort, needing.

I found a little white feather on the front drive this morning, a sign from Kevin because he knows these last weeks and months have been harder than ever. Christmas and New Year looming, but more so 9 February. There are no words.

I am collecting the feathers in Kevin's 'card money' tin. The tin brings back so many happy, fun memories of playing cards with family and friends. Kevin won many games as his tin was always heavy, but now it's heavy with comforting feathers.

Saturday, 19 December 2020

Sitting by the fireplace, crying my eyes out, I look up, and there is Bess with a ball. She's looking at me, maybe saying, 'Cmon, Mum. Stop crying. Let's play.' It hurts.

I play Kevin's music mix. 'Something to Believe In', by the Bangles. Is there, is there, Kevin? It's not fair. You were too young, too nice, and didn't deserve to die. You were told two to five years when diagnosed, why did you only get two? Wish we had done more living alongside the treatment, but I know it was difficult for you. I would say to anyone in our position to try to do that—more living. We really didn't. I should have pushed Kevin to do more, but it was hard, really hard.

Sunday, 20 December 2020

Our Janet is coming over to go to the drive-in carol singing service at the local swimming pool car park. It was different. If you had said a year ago we would be sitting in the car, in a car park, looking at a stage, and watching Christmas carol singing, well! The churches in the area got together to put this on.

Monday, 21 December 2020

Countdown to Christmas Day. I normally greet these days with excitement, listening to Christmas tunes on the radio, making notes of last-minute preparations, checking TV Christmas show viewing options. But there is none of that this year. It just feels numb, sad. I wish it was here and gone. I've got to cope, got to.

Tuesday, 22 December 2020

I'm in the car when 'Going Loco Down in Acapulco' comes on the radio. It's a lively, fun song, but I started crying because I looked at the picture that I have on my car visor of us, on a cruise in the sunshine. Made me think of the fun sail away days with music, drinks, and dancing, and it made me cry.

Kevin and Diane on a Cruise

Wednesday, 23 December 2020

I went to see Ian, Leanne, Grace, Jack, and Cookie. It was a really lovely few hours and a lovely chicken dinner. For once I didn't look at a meal and think, *I can't eat this*. Being with them all, I didn't think about it because I wasn't on my own.

Margaret was taken to St Georges Hospital.

Thursday, 24 December 2020, Christmas Eve

Margaret returned home. I went to the crematorium to lay Christmas flowers for Mum and Dad. I met the family there. I took hot chocolate; I think I just wanted to make them stay a bit longer and chat.

I went to the Christmas Eve service at St Peter's. Whoa, it was a frosty, icy evening going out in the car at 11.15 p.m.! There were not many there, but it gave me a comforting and warm feeling. I got home and carried on our tradition of salmon butty and sherry while sitting in front of the fire.

Friday, 25 December 2020, Christmas Day

It still feels numb. Christmas breakfast tradition of a hot turkey butty, but the oven doesn't cook as quickly as it should, so it wasn't ready for breakfast. So choccy biscuits then. Took the dogs out for a walk. I didn't really feel like putting on a red woolly Christmas hat, as I usually do when I walk the dogs on a Christmas morning, so I didn't. I came back, opened champagne and poured a glass each for us in our special champagne glasses. I drank both. I found another white feather in the hall, in the hall! Yes, so cheers, Kevin. I know you are with me. Gotta believe, and I do.

I spoke to the family, and Tommy and Amanda came round for a few hours midday. That was nice. They bought me a personalised 2021 photo calendar - photo memories of pictures of Kevin and I. Kevin always bought me a calendar. This year I was going to use the freebie IFAW one, but I won't now.

I probably drank too much champagne. I smothered the Christmas dinner in gravy and couldn't see what I was eating through tears. I gave up and opened the popcorn.

At 6 p.m., I joined our families' and friends' (each and all in their own homes, near and far) cheers to Kevin. Cheers, my lovely, bestest husband and friend. It hurts.

Went to bed at 9.15 p.m.

Saturday, 26 December 2020, Boxing Day

I managed to get through yesterday, sort of! OK, sofa time now, tree lights glowing, dogs sleeping after walk. I may even open another bottle of champagne. Why not?

Call the Midwife is on TV. It made me cry when they were having a Christmas gathering and unexpected friends arrived, but he just said, 'The more the merrier.' That was us. We loved having lots of people around too.

And then, the show talked about 'Strength has been tested too many times.' Don't want that to sound like me, but I feel it. I'm on the emotional edge. There are times when I just felt like getting in the car and driving off a bridge or jumping on a train line. Yes but no. Layla and Bess need me.

Now a bad, bad day, tears streaming. A sad time. Actually sitting on the toilet now crying my eyes out, crying! Again, who sits crying on a toilet? I need to get a grip. Is this normal in the grief process? When you lose the love of your life, that's the way it is. No one can help. There are no pills or potions to make you feel better. The way I see it is you just gotta get through each and every day and try to go forward. Yes, that sounds harsh, but it's true. Don't look for anyone to help make it better. They can't. Cry, cry. I don't want to bother family and friends because yes, they are all so there for me, but they can't take away the deep pain.

I opened the living room door as Layla, God bless her, was annoying me with her panting. Then I heard a dog toy squeak. It made me smile. Is that you, Kevin? I know it is, so I stop crying and calm down. You are with us.♥

Get a grip, played poker tonight with Ottershaw friends. I have to keep from saying anything sad in the chat area because they don't know how I feel. It's not their fault Kevin is not here.

Sunday, 27 December 2020

I went to work, just a four-hour shift. I'm not sleeping well, though, and my head is all over the place at the moment. There is a bad, horrible week looming. No one can help. I can't explain. This time last year we were nearing the time - 2 January - when Kevin went into hospital, and didn't come home. It hurts.

This is one of the worst weeks of my life over the past three years. It all comes flooding back from last year. Kevin was ill a few weeks before Christmas, sickness and more. Christmas Day he felt OK and got up and dressed. We ate some dinner together. It was good.

Then Boxing Day brought more sickness, green projectile vomit. He was so weak, there was brown water in his stoma bag. DNs could not help, and Macmillan advised speaking to our local doctor, who prescribed anti-sickness tablets. Really! Spoke to 111, but it was like a communication of war and peace with their procedures before they even got a doctor to phone Kevin. Then we had to relay all the symptoms and history again to the doctor. It was exhausting, upsetting. I was trying to help Kevin on my own, the doctor finally came out to see Kevin on the 2nd January, said he should go to hospital. So on 2 January, Kevin left home in an ambulance. I didn't know he wasn't coming home ever again.

The doctor said Kevin would go straight to a ward. He didn't. My heart broke for him. We spent over twelve hours in A&E before he got onto a ward. He didn't deserve that, but he was so humble. I'm crying as I write this. Actually, crying is an understatement. I feel like I hate this world.

Monday, 28 December 2020

I really don't want to go out the door this week, and until after, well, after New Year. I can't face talking to family and friends because I can't do the 'I'm OK.' I feel so low. Then my nephew, Ian, phoned and asks me to join them at Formby Beach. I am so glad he phoned, and I did. It lifted me up like I wouldn't have believed. I am strong. I have to do this for Kevin. I will. Thank you, Ian, Leanne, Grace, Jack, and Cookie. They also invited me to join them for a meal on New Year's Eve at 4 p.m. I immediately said yes. That's right, isn't it, Kevin, be positive?

Wednesday, 30 December 2020

Grief is like going through the motions of living. Looking down at your day, get up and go through the day, and then go to bed. Numb. Day after day, not actually living. Trying to smile, saying, 'I'm OK.' Laughing even.

I listen to Alicia Keys: 'If I aint got you … tears streaming because I haven't.'

Thursday, 31 December 2020

Meal is cancelled. We're in lockdown—again!

Margaret is not well. She goes by ambulance to St Raphael's Hospice. I'm on pins waiting for news. I'm so worried.

Tommy and Amanda come over for New Year's Eve. We have a few drinks. We talk about Kevin.

2021

Friday, 1 January 2021

I spoke to Colin. Margaret is 'comfortable'. I feel helpless but sort of relieved. I think it will help Colin that she is being cared for and in good hands. I had a PJ day. Just put waterproofs and a jumper on over them to take the dogs out. Who cares? My mind is elsewhere.

Saturday, 2 January 2021

I woke up and got dressed. I wondered, *When will I put PJs back on?* I was thinking about the meaning of life. The real meaning of my life, but that made me smile because then I thought of the Monty Python video box set (which we have). Kevin loved Monty Python's *The Meaning of Life.* Anyway, I need to do more in life, find a new job, a fresh start. Let's update CV.

I moved stuff around in the new shed to make space for my bike. As soon as brighter days are here I want to get out on my bike. I am also drawing landscape plan for garden. I want to grow stuff. The garden needs more colour.

I was thinking of family saying they are proud of me, that I'm strong. I don't feel it, but it feels good to hear them say it, and keeps me on that path.

Monday, 4 January 2021

I couldn't sleep last night. I woke up thinking about getting a smaller bed. I need to for it to fit better in the new bedroom. But I don't want to get rid of our bed. I am scared I will regret it. Is it too soon?

I feel low and scared about Margaret's results today.

I'm reading a clip of a real-life story on grief called, 'My Husband's Ashes.' I can relate to so much of it, like scattering ashes too far to visit. No, I'm not doing that. Kevin is staying right here with me.

Tuesday, 5 January 2021

Again, waiting on pins for news of Margaret. Colin phoned with bad news. The bloods show her liver is failing, and we need to be prepared. I told Colin I would speak with him again tomorrow evening. I so need to see Margaret, but there are so many COVID-19 hurdles. Can I travel? Can I stay at a Travelodge? Can I actually see her in the hospice? I checked on all those things before I told Colin I could get down to London. I'll leave at 9 a.m. tomorrow. I just want time with her to talk to her, not to say goodbye.

Wednesday, 6 January 2021

I set off for London at 9.30 a.m. After two hours on the road, I got a call from Elaine. Margaret had passed away. I got there at 1.30 p.m.; I missed seeing her alive by two hours. Why didn't I go last night? Why didn't

I go last weekend? Why? Because I thought she would come home with Macmillan support, and I would have had a chance to visit her there. I didn't.

When I got to the hospice, I sat with Margaret for a while, talking, reminiscing, playing Frank Sinatra's 'Summer Wind'. Will miss you so, so much.♥ Margaret, a special mum-in-law and the bestest mum to Kevin. Margaret, you look at peace, even smiling. You are, because you are with your 'little boy' again now.

RIP together with a Bacardi and Coke, laughing over a card game.♥ ♥

Saturday, 9 January 2021

I'm feeling so sad but then had zoom with Trish, for four hours! That definitely cheered me up. Thank you, Trish, for sharing lovely memories of Kevin, Margaret, and Colin.

In grief, we need to talk, to reminisce, to remember.

Time for some food, I think, and an evening with our lovely Bess and Layla. What's life about? What's life about?

Monday, 11 January 2021

I've been thinking about life in lockdown; living with grief, and the looming anniversary of losing Kevin. I'm an emotional wreck on the inside and a zombie on the outside.

Tuesday, 12 January 2021

I went to the beach today. It is lovely, peaceful, and blissful. I feel blessed when I am there, but Kevin is not there with us. So my head tells me it is lovely, but my heart tells me it is not.

Wednesday, 13 January 2021

I had an unusual dream last night. I was asleep, and it was dark in the bedroom. I always fall asleep holding 'Kevin', like a comfort blanket I suppose. I had the feeling of waking up, hearing voices, and of seeing shapes of four people in the darkness, whispering to each other. I said, 'What do you want? Go away'. Then I felt a hand hold my hand, which scared me. I woke myself up by shouting, 'Get off me!' I'm sorry if it was you, Kevin, perhaps with your mum and my mum and Dad too. The four closest people I have lost. I didn't mean to tell you to go away. I'm sorry. Please come back. I won't be afraid the next time.♥

Later in the day, I had a really nice Zoom, with the family. Then they were gone. After the Zoom, there was only me. It would have been me and Kevin. I feel alone.

Off to bed, feeling alone, trying not to cry in front of the dogs. I've told them, 'Bedtime, suppertime', all the usual schedule before bed. I went to the toilet and am sitting there crying. Again crying on the toilet. I really gotta stop this. I miss you so much Kevin. Come hold my hand again tonight please.♥

Friday, 15 January 2021

I finally received the grant of probate today after ten months! I don't understand why, when you have a Will and a Death Certificate, you have to pay the government £220 to issue you with a piece of paper to say you can deal with your husband's financial affairs. Isn't that what the Will is for, and the Death Certificate, and a Marriage Certificate? Calm down. I really just feel there is a lack of understanding and compassion with these government departments, and too much red tape.

Sunday, 17 January 2021

Had a family Zoom today. It was lovely. Then the same thing. I got upset when they had all gone, and it was just me, Bess, and Layla again. I played online poker with the OSC gang, so that cheered me up. Highs and lows, highs and lows of grief. After poker I hit a low. I put on our music, which mostly at the moment makes me cry and feel sad. I text Roz. She phoned me back and we talked. She knows.

Monday, 18 January 2021

Watched *Finding Alice*, a TV drama. The sadness, tears, and being awake at 4 a.m. only touches the tip of the iceberg of what it's really like to be a widow. It's much worse than the TV drama portrayed. The money issue that was raised was interesting. And it's true. Banks and other financial institutions could be, shall we say 'less blinkered'! The show did prompt a true saying: 'Pleasant times not things are important in life.'

Tuesday, 19 January 2021

Had a Zoom with Trish. A bit boozy but fun and lifting. Then jeepers, the same thing - finished the zoom, felt so sad, and cried.

Wednesday, 20 January 2021

I watched the US inauguration. President Joe Biden seems like a lovely, lovely man with the human touch like no other. He said, 'Unity, unity we are good people', and that he will be a president for all Americans. 'Defend the truth and defeat the lies … Life—there is no accounting for what fate will deal you.' That's so true.

I played quiz with the Haven gang. It was very good. No wine tonight and no crying.

Thursday, 21 January 2021

It's Elaine's birthday. She was pleased with delivery of a cake, balloon, wine, and a rose plant. I'm really glad. It made me feel happy to send it.

Friday, 22 January 2021

No wine, but I'm feeling sad. But I do feel like this bungalow is putting its arms around me, giving me a big, comfy hug, a big hug from Kevin. So I tell myself not to feel sad.

Saturday, 23 January 2021

I didn't sleep again last night. Hate it. Hate it.

Sunday, 24 January 2021

Joined the Ottershaw church zoom service. It made me smile when Jesus was referred to as a 'partygoer'. At least we have something in common.

Then I took a refreshing walk on the beach with Bess and Layla. It was really lovely.

Then a Zoom with the 'Welsh birds'- Fi and Julia, and Trick and Suze. It was really good to see them all. I enjoyed it, but I drank too much wine! But I need to because I miss you, Kevin. I miss you. I need you. It hurts, it hurts. I miss you, and it hurts.♥

Tuesday, 26 January 2021

It's our Janet's birthday. Family Zoom. It was good to see everyone. It ended too soon, but life goes on for all. Except for me.

Wednesday, 27 January 2021

Damn! About 9.30 p.m. there was a big bang in hall, and the lights went out. It was the hall ceiling light, and it blew the electric box. Why do these things happen in the dark? I took the light cover down, and the bulb had blown out of its holder, which was left in the ceiling! What do I do? What do I do?

Friday, 29 January 2021

COVD vaccine jab day. Then feeling the pain tonight. No, not the pain of the vaccination but the pain of losing Kevin. I often think about how it would have been different if you had gone through cancer treatment and being ill in hospital and the hospice, during COVID-19. A shiver runs down my spine. I can't imagine how people have coped with those situations during the lockdowns.

Sunday, 31 January 2021

I had eight hours of sleep last night for the first time since I don't know when. I was awake until about 3 a.m., got to sleep, and woke at 8 a.m. to let the dogs out. I went back to bed, thinking just for about an hour, and the next thing I knew, it was 11 a.m.!

Had a busy day. After a lovely walk with the dogs, I filled the holes in back of the kitchen cupboards (the area where the pipes come through) to stop Mickey Mouse from coming in; we have a mouse. Then I fixed the blown ceiling light.

Time for wine. And I fell asleep on the sofa. Then I heard Kevin ask, 'Are you coming to bed?' It was such a lovely, warm, comfy feeling. Then I woke up on the sofa, and he wasn't there.

Monday, 1 February 2021

Well. January is over. But I still woke up this morning with that sad feeling in the pit of my stomach, like most mornings really. A week to dread, to fear emotions. I reach over to hug 'Kevin' and tell myself I must get up and carry on with this day.

Tuesday, 2 February 2021

Margaret's funeral is on Friday. Kevin's anniversary is next Tuesday, the ninth, 11.15 a.m. I'm thinking about both all the time. It hurts. I swerve my thoughts, emotions, away to keep on top of it. I switch off my emotions.

Wednesday, 3 February 2021

I'm crying as I watch *Rich Holiday, Poor Holiday*. A woman on a poor holiday said she and her daughter and grandkids are there for each other. I don't have that now that I've lost Kevin, we havn't got each other.

It was a bad evening – our music, wine and lots of tears. Can't believe you are gone, Kevin. You were not meant to go. Why, why, why?

Thursday, 4 February 2021

I'm on the road to London. Margaret's funeral is tomorrow.

I felt so alone checking into the Travelodge without Kevin, but I need to get used to this. I put a chair up against the door because my room was down a long corridor, and I was scared It is just me now.

Friday, 5 February 2021

It's the day of Margaret's funeral.

It was really hard. It's so, so sad that Margaret has gone. It was also the first funeral for me since Kevin's. Seeing the coffin was just too much. I did cry for you, Margaret, but I cried buckets for Kevin.

COVID-19 means Margaret's friends cannot join us for the wake. Perhaps there will be a memorial next year. I cannot imagine not being able to have done a farewell for Kevin.

Margaret, you are in my heart always and forever. Thank you for the lovely memories, good times, and for having Kevin as a son, who became my husband.

Saturday, 6 February 2021

I feel alone. I just need to get home to the dogs.

Sunday, 7 February 2021

Waking up hurts, it hurts. I'm scared. I try not to think of you, Kevin. It sounds awful, but it stops the hurt, the pain, the sadness. I'm scared where it will take me. I need to get through the next few days, up to and including the anniversary of losing you, Kevin. I just need to try to keep sane. Bess and Layla help so much. Let's go to the beach.

So close to wanting to be with you tonight. I want to be with you, Kevin. I'm sitting here tears streaming. There is no way forward, no life that I need without you. I can't hurt myself. I wish I could just close my eyes and not wake up, but I know you wouldn't want me to do that. And then I look at our dogs. I need to be here for them.

Monday, 8 February 2021

Last night was closest I've come to wanting to join you, Kevin. It was a different hurt. It was more in my head than my body. And I've got a pain over my right eye and pains in my head, like a headache but not a headache.

I get on with a normal day, but every step of the day I was thinking about this time last year, that horrible, horrible discussion we had with the doctor around 12 p.m. It needed to be had, I know, but not fair. The doctor was so nice, and you were so brave. But I couldn't accept what the outcome would be. You were never dying.❤

Tuesday, 9 February 2021

A year ago today you closed your eyes forever.

I dreamt again last night of lying in the darkness, and you tried to hug me. I was scared. I'm learning. Please come back.

Our love and the memories of our special life together help me to get through each and every day, especially today. I browse through our pictures of treasured memories. All these memories keep me going.

I will love and miss you always and forever.

Wednesday, 10 February 2021

I've been off social media for a few days. I can't cope. I can only deal with my thoughts and memories. Mary Wilson from the Supremes died yesterday, so I'm listening to that lovely music, 'Baby Love'. Been to the beach with Bess and Layla.

Thursday, 11 February 2021

I saw 4 a.m. again last night. I was falling asleep on the sofa, and then as soon as I go to bed, I'm wide awake. Could not lie in, but will take some Nytol tonight as I'm going to work tomorrow and don't want to be up until 4 a.m. again.

I woke up this morning, my mind is full. Life is dark, like in a dark train tunnel, but going nowhere. And there is not even a chink of light.

Saturday, 13 February 2021

Tommy and Amanda came over for a few hours this evening. We had a very nice chat, it was good to get together. I'm OK about tomorrow, Valentine's Day. It's filled with happy memories of Valentines past. I feel I'll get through that day better than other special dates of the year.

Sunday, 14 February 2021

I got out all our past valentine cards and put them on Kevin's chair. We mostly celebrated at the OSC with our friends, which we both enjoyed, so there was no meal for two to be sad about not having. We both thought it was overrated to do that on the fourteenth, but we always bought cards for each other, always, and flowers and chocs. Kevin, my lovely, funny Valentine always and forever.♥

Kevin - my valentine

Monday, 15 February 2021

I am feeling OK today. I dread that sad feeling, that horrible sadness deep inside, touching every fibre of my body. My whole body consumed with sadness.

Watching news about the duchess of Sussex, and she mentioned 'unbearable grief'. I feel that way too.

Tuesday, 16 February 2021

I must phone Colin. I couldn't phone last week; I couldn't really speak to anyone. It was a bad week. I so wanted to join you, Kevin. Then I looked at four eyes watching me and knew I can't leave them.

Wednesday, 17 February 2021

I went to Tesco today. I got there, parked up, and realised I had forgotten my purse!

Thursday, 18 February 2021

Oddly, I'm feeling upbeat today. The sun is shining, the sky is blue, and the clouds are fluffy white. Life is for living. I've got to.

Popped into Susan and Tommy's for a social distance sandwich. Then I dropped some birthday gifts off at Ian's. It was nice to see them all, even socially distanced.

Yes, I've got to stop crying. I try to keep that horrible sad feeling at bay by telling myself, 'Don't let it get you. Life is for living.'

Friday, 19 February 2021

I'm exhausted from crying and feeling sad and alone. I've got to tell myself to stop, stop. I've got a lot to live for, I hope, and I've got to live. Driving to work today, I drove past my turn off exit - concentrate!

Saturday, 20 February 2021

Different days! I was trying to be positive yesterday, and I'm crying again today looking at our cruise pictures. We should have had a lot more like that to look forward to.

Sunday, 21 February 2021

It's horrible reaching out in bed, and you are not there.

Tuesday, 23 February 2021

It's difficult. You don't want to, and you say, 'Right. Not drinking this week. Wait until the weekend.' Then midweek, the strip light in the utility room goes. Is it the starter, or is it the tube? Something daft, unimportant, but it hits the sensitive nerves of emotion, and I need a drink!

So I go and buy both a tube and a starter. I don't want to get home with a new starter, and it's the tube, or vice versa. It was the tube. It was a job to get the cover off. Not the end of the world but big in my sad world. Hey, done it. It's working again now.

Sunday, 28 February 2021

Sort of an OK day. I pottered in the garden on this sunny day. I played poker online and made a ping dinner.

Then I couldn't eat it. I cried and cried. It hurts. I just want Kevin back. I fear too much wine didn't help my emotions. Then Bess brought me a gift, her tennis ball. It made me smile. Thanks, Kevin.♥

Monday, 1 March 2021

It's March, and I am feeling better today. Had a nice visit for cuppa from Susan and Tommy. I didn't mention any of yesterday. No point.

Thursday, 4 March 2021

I'm keeping busy and don't feel as scared or upset about tomorrow as other 'firsts' this year. I think it's because I feel grateful we could give Kevin the farewell, fitting tribute, he deserved. So many others haven't been able to do that this horrible year due to COVID-19, Margaret included. It's so sad.

Friday, 5 March 2021

Kevin, you're in my thoughts every second of every minute of every hour of today.♥

I received comforting thoughts from family and friends. Thank you all.

Monday, 8 March 2021

Listening to music - 'Heaven Must Have Sent You' by the Elgins is a lovely song. It certainly sent you to me, Kevin.

Tuesday, 9 March 2021

Watching *Your Honor*, a TV drama. A clip shows the funeral car going past the home of the deceased, as a mark of respect. The scene upset me as I remembered we did that for you, Kevin. We slowed down at Slade Road, on your last journey past it.

Then I thought of the times we walked in and out of the drive at Slade Road—to go to the club, to the Indian spicy otter restaurant, to the Castle pub, to Miller & Carter. It made me sad to think of all those journeys and then this journey. But I'm so glad the cars slowed down. I wouldn't have thought about it, and now I remember us slowing down as clear as day. I appreciate the respectful gesture and treasure the memory.

Tuesday, 16 March 2021

How is it when someone you love dies, you look at things with more thought. Going through Kevin's holiday albums I found photos of his skiing trip to Kitzbuhel, Austria. I'd seen them before, but it just seems that the things you knew when they were alive seemed in the past, but when they are gone, their past is part of your present. I think I will walk in your footsteps and go there; I think it would be comforting. Or should I say ski in your footsteps, although from your account of the holiday, it was more après-ski!♥

Friday, 19 March 2021

It's our Tommy's birthday. I popped round for birthday cuppa. There will be lots of celebrations to catch up on after COVID-19.

Got home and watched Red Nose Day. It finished with the song 'Smile' by Gabrielle: 'When there are clouds in the sky you'll get by, light up your face with gladness, hide every trace of sadness. Smile, what's the use of crying, you'll find that life is still worthwhile, If you just smile.' Yes, we all need to.

Saturday, 20 March 2021

Driving home from work, a Seekers song from February 1965 came on the radio: 'I still need you there beside me, no matter what I do, for I know I'll never find another you.' So true, so true. It made me cry.

Sunday, 21 March 2021

What to do? What to do? To the beach with the dogs. Blissful.

Phoned Susan and went round for a cuppa. I also bumped into Ian, Leanne, and the kids. It was lovely to see them, lovely.

Got home and I sat in the garden, although cold!. But it was just good to sit in the daylight with our girlies, Kevin.

Sitting on the sofa last night, Facebook pinged with a lovely local restaurant offering 'order and collect'. So I ordered a lamb roast dinner. Sort of a click and collect. A bit lazy, but why not. So, all I had to do was open the wine. Dinner very tasty. But like so many other times, I couldn't eat most of it as you are not here to sit and eat with me. I miss you, start crying. Layla nudged my leg. Bess came up to me, and then off she went to find the tennis ball and brought it back to me. I smiled through my tears.

Wednesday, 24 March 2021

It was a bright, sunny day. Our Tommy came over and mowed the lawn, the first mow at Watchyard Lane. Then Susan and Tommy came round for a cuppa, which turned into a red wine. Nice. After they left, I sat in Kevin's chair with wine, looking into the garden, listening to *Among the Living*. The poker What's App pinged, and I had a great game with lovely friends. Followed by a cry with a sherry.

Thursday, 25 March 2021

Sleepless night and work tomorrow! Hot milk and thoughts at 3 a.m.

Life: I'm holding on, but for what purpose, I don't know.

Friday, 26 March 2021

On the way home from work, the song on the radio 'Get along without you now' makes me cry. I can't get along without you. I can't.

Saturday, 27 March 2021

Working today. Our Janet is coming over to stay tonight. That will be nice. But driving home from work, again I'm crying. A bad week is ahead with Kevin's and Margaret's birthdays and Colin and Margaret's wedding anniversary.

I should not listen to smooth radio on the drive home from work. It makes me cry every time.

Tuesday, 30 March 2021

I went to visit Sharon. Today's her birthday. We spent a lovely afternoon in the garden with her family. It was really nice.

I spoke to Colin when I got home. The whisky and whisky fudge I sent to him had arrived. I just wanted to send him a little 'toast' for their sixtieth wedding anniversary on 1 April. Though Margaret will not be here to celebrate with Colin, she will always be with him. They had sixty years together.

Wednesday, 31 March 2021

Went to visit Susan and Tommy. The kids were there, and we had a lovely few hours.

Thursday, 1 April 2021

Cheers to Colin and Margaret, sixty years wed today. Sat with a drink to toast them and listened to 'Summer Wind' playing.

I can't help saying I wish I had sixty years with my Kevin.♥ But I know the time we did have was precious, like any time we have with the ones we love.

It hurts. It hurts to listen to David Bowie's 'Heroes'. Also, the song, 'Everything Means Nothing if I Ain't Got You', the words of that song are so true, so true.♥

Saturday, 3 April 2021

Happy birthday, Kevin! XXX♥ ♥ ♥

Champagne later when I get home from work. Our Tommy came over and joined me for the usual Indian meal Kevin and I always went out for on our birthdays.

Sunday, 4 April 2021

Bernie arrived. It was really great to see him, and we had a lovely catchup. I felt quite emotional. His mum lives in Manchester, so he travelled up from Ottershaw on Friday to visit her and came across today. Really lovely.

Monday, 5 April 2021

Happy birthday, Margaret. Remembered always. XXX

Sunday, 11 April 2021

Worked yesterday and Friday. Having a quiet weekend for the week ahead, a build up to my second COVID-19 jab on Friday, 16 April.

What's App pinged from the poker gang. Yes please ill play. I also had a nice chat with Pam G this afternoon.

I'm trying to keep positive, though I am feeling down listening to the song 'Where Do Broken Hearts Go' playing on the radio. And like the lyrics, 'I don't know, I don't know.' I don't where to go. I sat in Kevin's chair, tears streaming. I miss Kevin so, so much.

Then the song, 'Rains Down in Africa'. Take the time to do things. Can I? I will. I must.

Tuesday, 13 April 2021

I went to see a kennel today, nice size for each dog, but no grass run attached to each kennel, but none of them have, the staff are really nice. I'd love to build my own kennels, where the 'cells' would be more like a luxury flat, with a grass run in each.

I need a drink! I had chat with Colin and a nice Zoom with Pam S. Played Haven poker in the evening, had great fun and it perked me up. It was a great game with great friends. Had another drink. Who cares? I don't. What is life?

Wednesday, 14 April 2021

Today is a better day. The carpenter phoned me about making a front gate. The front door is at the side of the house, I worry when I open it to let the dogs out to go to the car because I can't see the road, so with a gate on, they can't run out into the road. Updating my CV, again thinking of changing my job. Zoom quiz tonight with the Haven gang.

Friday, 16 April 2021

Had my second jab. In two weeks time, I should have a good immunity from COVID-19. Little steps to some sort of normal life again. Tommy stayed over. It was a nice evening. And the bestest news was that he and Amanda are getting married next year. Something to look forward to. I am so pleased and happy for them.

Saturday, 17 April 2021

Prince Philip, Duke of Edinburgh's funeral is at Windsor Castle chapel today. Very poignant, when the green Land Rover hearse came through the arch to collect Prince Phillip's coffin. Just seeing that made me feel there is a green Land Rover coming for us all one day. The Queen sat on her own, but even if family were seated next to her, I know she would still feel alone, because you do.

Monday, 19 April 2021

Today is Susan's birthday. Last year I did not leave home to go and see her because I was totally scared of COVID-19. But this year is another year. We have the vaccine, I have had the jabs, and life restarts. It's Becci's birthday too will celebrate that in due course.☺

Had a lovely afternoon in Susan's garden with the family. So much so I decided to leave the car, and take a taxi home. But I could not get a taxi. And as I'm still an emotional wreck, and more so after a few drinks, I just sobbed, sobbed. I need to stop crying; it's not their fault Kevin is not with me. I don't want them to worry about me. I just need to get home to Bess and Layla. Just needed to get home.

How can you have such a lovely afternoon with sis, celebrating her birthday, and then cry so much? Sometimes, I feel so sad behind the smiles. I feel sad because I miss Kevin so much. I got home and cried more. I looked at myself in the mirror. Get a grip, girl!

At 9 p.m., I'm sitting on my own. I can't watch TV. I can't concentrate. It's music time. Sitting here, I'm not afraid of dying. I've really got nothing to live for without you, Kevin. But I can't, I can't. I need to look after Bess and Layla.

About 10.25, I dozed off on the sofa. When I woke, for thirty seconds, I don't know what day or time it is. Then I realise you are not here. Time for bed for us three.

Grief has a lingering aftershock, a long, long, lingering aftershock.

I'm still collecting white feathers. They seem to appear when I'm down and sad, thinking of you. They are building up in your 'card money tin', the tin with pictures of teddies on it.☺♥

Wednesday, 21 April 2021

It's Queen Elizabeth's ninety-fifth birthday. There is a lot on TV about her first birthday without Prince Philip. She will cope. We all have to.

Friday, 23 April 2021

The weekend looms. Weekends are hard, although I'm working most of Saturday. Then Sunday happens, then Monday, and so on.

Watched *Gogglebox*. Jeepers, if you need a distraction and a good old belly laugh, that's the programme to watch. Therapy at its best.

Saturday, 24 April 2021

Well after getting home and realising what I said about weekends yesterday, our Tommy text to say he and Amanda will pop over tomorrow, early evening. I thought I had forgotten about an arrangement, but I hadn't. He just text to say they would pop over. Isn't that weird. Here I am, thinking I gotta get through Saturday. But Sunday won't be so bad now.

Sunday, 25 April 2021

Had a lovely visit with Tommy and Amanda. I had my little book with quips I'd noted from *Gogglebox* to share with them only because when I watch it, I laugh out loud and miss sharing that with Kevin. So I shared a laugh with them.

Tuesday, 27 April 2021

Played poker with the Haven gang this evening and had a really good time. But then I listened to music, 'Our Life Together……..(John Lennon)'. Nice time and then sad time - highs and lows. Got to move forward, putting one foot in front of the other. There is pain, but there is love, and there is hope.

I don't think I can carry on with this job. I wake up and dread going to work. It's not the staff or some parts of the job. It's the thought of stepping back into a world that was part of the worst time of my life. I started there six months before Kevin was diagnosed with cancer, and I and worked after the terminal diagnosis, during the chemo, after losing Kevin, and during the lockdown, while on my own in grief.

I don't sleep well the night before I have to work, and then I'm tired at work. My head is saying leave; my heart is saying stay. It's a tussle of emotions. They have been so supportive, and I don't want to let them down. I struggle with thinking about whether I should have left the job before and spent more time with you. I'm sorry, Kevin, I'm sorry. (I finally resigned from this job in June 2021.)

May 2021

Some days I feel low; some days I don't feel low. To have had someone in your life, someone so special, and with whom you have experienced happy, fun, and loving times, then the days after they are not with you, can be low or not so low, depending on what memories are with you that day. Each day, you don't know how you will feel, and what might or might not upset you.

It's a comfort to sleep in Kevin's recliner chair. It feels like a big hug, so sometimes I drag the duvet and pillow off the bed and I settle down to sleep in Kevin's chair by the window, looking into the garden and up at the stars in the sky.

June 2021

It is nice to sit in our garden in Formby, quietly listening to the sounds around me; birds singing, families and children in gardens - life carrying on. I'm having a few glasses of wine because, because I can. Because I miss you so much. I get upset and start crying. Bess looks at me. Again, that look of, 'Where is dad?' I can't explain it to you, but Kevin is with us now, always, and forever.

Something I wanted to share as part of this book – Where's Layla:-

In December 2019, the family did secret santa gifts. Little did I know that Kevin drew me to buy a gift for. He bought me the fun book - Where's Layla – a funny adaption to the where's wally book series. They are available to buy on-line, you just download a picture of your dog and a book is produced. Each page has various scenes, but all hiding Layla. It was such a special final Christmas gift, even more so when on 8th February 2020, Kevin asked me to hand him the book and he wrote such special words on the inside cover.

(photo of book front cover and insert of what Kevin wrote)

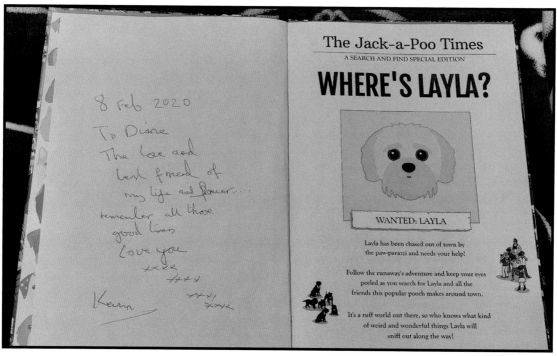

5

The End of the Diary

At some point I have to stop writing and repeating myself. My heart is broken. I can't stop crying; I know I always will. The hurt is no less, but the intervals between the sadness are fewer.

During the years from Kevin's cancer diagnosis and the chemo treatment, I feared dying myself and was scared. It was not because of dying, but because I was worried about who would look after Kevin, Layla, and Bess. This fear weighed heavily on my mind all the time. But then I lost Kevin, and the fear turned to my whole body being consumed by emotional, sad pain. 'Sad' seems such a short word for such an intense feeling and emotional heartbreak.

Whitney Houston asked, 'Where do broken hearts go?' I know the song is more apt to be about a break-up, but those words alone have me in tears because my heart is broken. The Beach Boys sang, 'God only knows … What good would living do me?' What can I say?

I've locked the door to my heart and shut it away. Only being with you again, one day, Kevin, will unlock it.

And so, Kevin, my whole being, my everything in life, thank you for being in Staines rugby club that night back in November 1991.

'Better to have loved and lost, than never to have loved at all.' I'm not sure I totally agree with that saying because I didn't want to lose you. You shouldn't have died, my sweetheart.

As Kevin would say to me at bedtime, 'Night dols.' I would reply, 'Night, night, sweetheart.' ♥

(A Christmas Star)

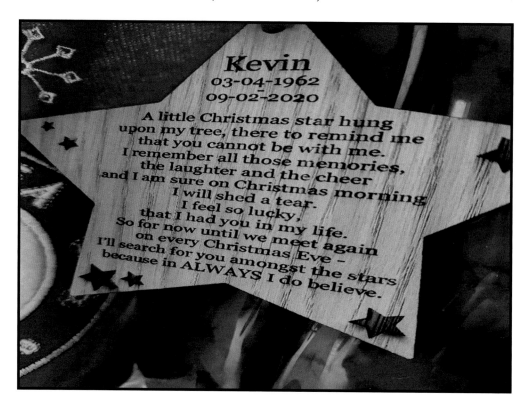

Kevin's ashes in the blue teardrop urn with his star, CFC Christmas hat, and a photo of us.

Skip, a border collie, February 1994–October 2007.

Sky, a blue merle collie, October 2007–July 2010.

Layla, a Jackapoo (Jack Russell/poodle), October 2009, and Bess, a working Collie, March 2011.

About the Author

I have never written a book before, and it is a diary really that is pulled together as a book. It was my way of 'talking' to someone, but not – ie. writing it down.

I have worked as a personal assistant/secretary for most of my life with a brief three-year period when I worked as an air stewardess; that was an amazing experience. It was shortly after I left the airlines that I met Kevin.

Over the years I have done voluntary work, mostly with animals. I volunteered at the RSPCA for over ten years down South, until I moved up North. I then volunteered for the Cinnamon Trust, a charitable organisation that helps elderly people who are physically unable to walk their dogs. The trust arranges for volunteers, like me, to walk their beloved, family members.

I presently volunteer at a local hospice a few hours a week.

Printed in the United States
by Baker & Taylor Publisher Services